Nursery Room: Discipleship Activities for 2 and 3 year olds

Author:
Teodora Mery Flores de Castañeda

Support and Advice Team:
Flor Ramírez Labrín
Josefa Chunga Zapata
Lady Valer Ramos
María Esther Sosa Alzamora
Elizabeth Sosa Alzamora
Ruth María Estrada Martínez

Revision and Adaptation by the SAM Region SDMI:
Mery Asenjo
Elizabeth Cristiana Soto Venegas
Ana Asenjo
Waleska Rios Sepulveda

Coordinator of the editorial project:
Patricia Picavea

Cover Design and Layout:
Slater Designer / Slater J. Chavez

Translated from Spanish to English:
Bethany Cyr

Edited by: Monte Cyr

ISBN: 978-1-63580-176-7

Copyright © 2020 by Iglesia del Nazareno Producciones SAM

Printed by:
Mesoamerica Region Discipleship Ministries
www.Discipleship.MesoamericaRegion.org

An electronic version of this book and other resources is available at:
www.SdmiResources.MesoamericaRegion.org

PREPARATION FOR TEACHERS

ACTIVITIES FOR BOYS AND GIRLS TWO TO THREE YEARS OLD

UNIT I:	Thank You, God, for Everything You've Done 3
UNIT II:	Knowing and Enjoying What God Has Created 43
UNIT III:	Knowing the Body That God Created for Me 83
UNIT IV:	Jesus Is My Friend, He Takes Care of Me Wherever I Go ... 123
APPENDIX	Sunday School / Christian Education Materials for Children....164

UNIT 1

THANK YOU, GOD, FOR EVERYTHING YOU'VE DONE

WEEK 1:	GOD MADE THE LIGHT	4
WEEK 2:	GOD MADE THE WATER	7
WEEK 3:	GOD MADE THE PLANTS	10
WEEK 4:	GOD MADE THE SUN	13
WEEK 5:	GOD MADE THE MOON	16
WEEK 6:	GOD MADE THE FISH	19
WEEK 7:	GOD MADE THE BIRDS	22
WEEK 8:	GOD MADE THE ANIMALS	25
WEEK 9:	GOD MADE A MAN	28
WEEK 10:	GOD MADE A WOMAN	31
WEEK 11:	THANK YOU, GOD, FOR DADDY & MOMMY	34
WEEK 12:	THANK YOU, GOD, FOR COLORS	37
WEEK 13:	MY GOD MADE EVERYTHING BEAUTIFUL	40

LESSON 1: GOD MADE THE LIGHT

Biblical Basis:
Genesis 1:1-5

Objective:
To understand that God made the light, and be thankful.

Class Preparation:
Teachers should meet beforehand to pray for the Class Preparation time. Then they should carefully read and reflect on Genesis 1:1-5.

Introduction

Carefully observe the following:

- What does the verse from the Bible Basis teach us?
- God made everything beautiful.
- He first made the light to give light to the universe.
- God's love was expressed in everything he did.
- God made a very beautiful world.
- God's purpose was to give us happiness.
- The world was created by a living God.
- At first, the earth was messy and empty.
- Darkness covered the earth.
- Because God made everthing, we recognize that he is our Creator. And the children can also learn this.
- God separated the day from the night.
- The light God made has effect throughout the earth and the cosmos.

Reflection

God is the light and has given us his heavenly and spiritual light to shine in our lives and bring and radiate light to these little ones. Let's pray, thanking God for the light he has given us, and let's seek to bless others with that spiritual light.

As you end your time together, prepare the materials for the class.

IMPORTANT INFORMATION:

THEME: GOD MADE THE LIGHT
BIBLE SCRIPTURE: Genesis 1:1-5

CLASS DEVELOPMENT:

Receive the boys and girls, taking their ages into account. Babies should be placed in cribs, playpens, on blankets or mats — depending on the classroom conditions. Then, welcome all the boys and girls, and indicate where the areas of play and other activities are (this is only for infants from 18 months). In this way, you can make sure that they'll be able to access the previously arranged material in an environment and at a suitable height for their age. This will also allow them to be able to share with their friends and teachers.

At the end of the play/activity time, gather all the children together, making a circle to pray and sing some songs to God, thus starting the lesson of the day.

Let's Talk. Say to the children, "A long time ago there was only darkness. God, who can do everything, decided to do something different. So one day he said, 'Let there be light!'"

After telling them this, talk about it with them, "And do you know what happened, next? … There was light and everything became bright! God called it 'Day.' How good it is to have light! When there is light, we can run, walk, skip, and we don't stumble because we can see clearly. But there was still darkness, and God called the darkness 'Night.' Our God is so good!"

Let's Play. Prepare ahead of time a shoe box that's painted black on the inside and green on the outside. Glue a drawing of creation to the inside of the box. This will be an example to help the little ones understand creation. Then, make a hole in the top of the box and another in one side (but cover the holes to begin with). Allow the children to look through the top hole only. Ask them, "Can you see anything?" Then, uncover the hole that was made in the side and shine a flashlight into the box. Tell the children to look again through the hole at the top. They will be able to see the drawing of creation that's inside the box.

Let's Learn. Emphasize that God — who can do anything — made the light. So today we can say, "Thank You, God, for what You did."

Activity. Give each student a worksheet (see the next page). Help the children cut or tear strips of light blue or white paper. Help them glue the strips of paper between the lines of the picture. The paper strips will simulate rays of light.

Conclusion. Invite the children to smile and thank God for these blessings received.

GOD MADE THE LIGHT

Instructions
Cut or tear strips of light blue or white paper and glue them on the picture between the lines to be the rays of light.

LESSON 2: GOD MADE THE WATER

Biblical Basis: Genesis 1:6-8

Objective: To understand that God separated the waters.

Class Preparation: Teachers should meet beforehand to pray for the Class Preparation time. Then they should carefully read and reflect on Genesis 1:6-8.

Introduction

Carefully observe the following:

- What do the verses from the Bible Basis teach us?
- On the second day, God created the water, the clouds, and the seas.
- God created a balanced world.
- Everything God made is beautiful: water, air, etc. All of these are very useful and indispensable in the life of human beings.
- We cannot live without air. We may lack other things and life can continue, but without air, life would never be possible.
- We must take care of the environment.
- Water is another indispensable element; therefore, we must take care of it by avoiding the contamination of our water sources, streams, rivers, oceans, etc.

Reflection

God, in his infinite wisdom, created a universe that gives us happiness. It makes us happy and grateful human beings.

Everything that God created is excellent and perfect.

God is the infinite creator of water. Our planet is made up of three quarters water; therefore, the planet needs water.

Let's take care of everything that God created.

Let's pray for the water, the air, and the earth that he created that are indispensable elements in our life. Let's also pray for the boys and girls in our class, that they'll always be grateful and recognize God as the giver of everything.

As you end your teacher preparation time together, prepare the materials for the class.

IMPORTANT INFORMATION:

THEME: GOD MADE THE WATER
BIBLE SCRIPTURE: Genesis 1:6-8

CLASS DEVELOPMENT:

Receive the boys and girls, taking their ages into account. Babies should be placed in cribs, playpens, on blankets or mats — depending on the classroom conditions. Then, welcome all the boys and girls, and indicate where the areas of play and other activities are (this is only for infants from 18 months). In this way, you can make sure that they'll be able to access the previously arranged material in an environment and at a suitable height for their age. This will also allow them to be able to share with their friends and teachers.

At the end of the play/activity time, gather all the children together, making a circle to pray and sing some songs to God, thus starting the lesson of the day.

Let's Talk. (Prepare ahead of time a cardboard circle 30 cm in diameter, and paint one side black and the other side light blue.) Show the children the cardboard circle and ask the following, "What is this?" (Allow the children to respond and listen carefully to their responses.) Then show the black side of the circle and ask the boys and girls to say together, "Everything was dark, and God said 'Let there be light.'" Then, show the blue side, and ask the little ones to say, "Everything was bright and there was lots of water. God is very wise."

Let's Play. Encourage children to play a game. Form two groups. One group will represent the raindrops and the other group, the clouds. Then tell them that when you say "Rain" the clouds will sit down and the raindrops will jump up and down. Do this a couple of times and then have the groups switch — the raindrops are now clouds and the clouds are raindrops. Say "Rain" again allowing the new raindrops to jump up and down.

Let's Learn. Remind children that God is very wise; he perfectly separated the water by placing it below and by placing the sky above.

Activity. Give each student a copy of the worksheet from the next page. Help them glue cotton onto the clouds to make them look fluffy. Then have them draw along the dotted lines and color their pictures.

Conclusion. Pray with the children and thank God for his love that he expresses in different ways. (If you can find a song or rhyme about rain, teach it to the children before your prayer time.)

GOD MADE THE WATER

Instructions
Glue cotton onto the clouds in the picture to make the clouds fluffy; draw along the dotted lines to form the waves and color your picture.

LESSON 3: GOD MADE THE PLANTS

Biblical Basis:
Genesis 1:11-13

Objective:
To understand that God made plants to help us.

Class Preparation:
Teachers should meet beforehand to pray for the Class Preparation time. Then they should carefully read and reflect on the verses listed under the Biblical Basis.

Introduction

Let's think about this carefully: This theme is related to the third day of creation. God, in his infinite love and power, created a different part of the world every day until he perfected the most suitable world in which his creations would receive a wonderful blessing, to have a balanced life. We must always be very grateful.

God gathered the waters to form oceans, lakes, and rivers. Then the dry land appeared. This land was suitable for plants, animals, and human life.

In Isaiah 41:19-20, a variety of plants that God created are mentioned, and through the ages, the benefits of many of them have been discovered. All, or almost all, are very useful, and their parts are used in different ways to provide for human needs. Here, we will mention some kinds of plants according to their uses:

Medicinal plants
Nutritious plants
Industrial plants
Ornamental plants

"… the hand of Jehovah has done this, … the Holy One of Israel has created it." (Isaiah 41:20).

Reflection

Plants are important and indispensable. They produce and release oxygen into the air, so we cannot live without them.

In John 15:1-2, Jesus teaches us — through a metaphor — about the importance of plants using the comparison of an element of his creation with the faithfulness of his children.

Pray, thanking our God for the wonderful things he has done, especially for creating plants. And let's also pray for the children in your class, that they'll recognize God as their Creator.

At the end of your teacher preparation time, prepare the materials for the lesson.

IMPORTANT INFORMATION:

THEME: GOD MADE THE PLANTS
BIBLE SCRIPTURE: Genesis 1:11-13

CLASS DEVELOPMENT:

Receive the boys and girls, taking their ages into account. Babies should be placed in cribs, playpens, on blankets or mats — depending on the classroom conditions. Then, welcome all the boys and girls, and indicate where the areas of play and other activities are (this is only for infants from 18 months). In this way, you can make sure that they'll be able to access the previously arranged material in an environment and at a suitable height for their age. This will also allow them to be able to share with their friends and teachers.

At the end of the play/activity time, gather all the children together, making a circle to pray and sing some songs to God, thus starting the lesson of the day.

Let's Talk. Bring some live flowers to class and show them to the children. Then ask the children if they have ever seen flowers; if they have a garden at home; and if they know the names of different kinds of trees. It is important that during this time of conversation, all the children participate and that they are listened to carefully.

Next, tell the children that flowers are all different colors: red, yellow, blue, etc. And ask them what God created after he created the water. If the children do not give the correct answer, tell them it was the plants. End this section by noting that God is indeed very wise.

Let's Play. Take some small potted plants to class. Give a watering can to each child so that they can add water to the seedlings. Then ask them: who made the plants? Teach them the rhyme "I'll Plant A Little Seed" by Miss Bekka, Children's Library (search on YouTube).

Let's Learn. Remind children that God is very wise and loving, and he is the one who created the plants because he loves us very much.

Activity. The week before class, ask parents to send various kinds of tree leaves with their children. During class, give each child a worksheet and instruct them to glue the leaves they brought onto the picture of the tree.

Conclusion. Pray to God, giving thanks for his wonderful creation and for the food that comes from plants.

GOD MADE THE PLANTS

Instructions
Glue the leaves you brought onto the tree picture.

LESSON 4: GOD MADE THE SUN

Biblical Basis:
Genesis 1:14-19

Objective:
To know about the sun and realize that God created it.

Class Preparation:
Teachers should meet beforehand to pray for the Class Preparation time. Then they should carefully read and reflect on Genesis 1:14-19.

Introduction

Carefully observe the following:

What does the Bible Basis tell us? ... It tells us that God created the sun, the moon, and the stars to benefit his creation. He also established day and night and ordered the sun to shine during the day and the moon to shine at night. The creation of the sun and moon also established the seasons of the year.

There are thousands of stars in the sky. The sun is a large star. This star is essential and must be healthy in order for there to be life on earth. Without it, there would be no heat or light, so earth would be cold and dark. Heat and light are produced by the sun.

This star that we call the sun is far from earth, but its rays reach us in a few minutes.

How amazing is God who made everything beautiful for us!

Reflection

We recognize God as our only Creator, and all of creation helps us recognize that he is the only God. He himself saw that everything was good. Let's be grateful to our Lord, like the Jews were when they celebrated with feasts in gratitude to God for their harvests.

The stars are indicators of day, night, the seasons, the time, and the calendar. Let's pray to the Lord and thank him for his creation, and ask him for wisdom as to how we can share his amazing works with our students.

At the end of your preparation time, prepare the materials for your class.

IMPORTANT INFORMATION:

THEME: GOD MADE THE SUN
BIBLE SCRIPTURE: Genesis 1:14-19

CLASS DEVELOPMENT:

Receive the boys and girls, taking their ages into account. Babies should be placed in cribs, playpens, on blankets or mats — depending on the classroom conditions. Then, welcome all the boys and girls, and indicate where the areas of play and other activities are (this is only for infants from 18 months). In this way, you can make sure that they'll be able to access the previously arranged material in an environment and at a suitable height for their age. This will also allow them to be able to share with their friends and teachers.

At the end of the play/activity time, gather all the children together, making a circle to pray and sing some songs to God, thus starting the lesson of the day.

Let's Talk. Present some pictures of the sun (big and small), and ask the little ones, "Do you know what this is? What is it called? (Wait for the children to express themselves) … It's the sun! Who made the sun? What does the sun give us? The sun warms us, makes the plants grow and gives us light. It appears very early in the morning and then hides at night. Everything that God made is good. He is very wise."

Let's Play. Ask all the boys and girls to close their eyes. Then say, "Everything was dark and God spoke. He said, 'Let there be light', and the light came." Then, ask the children to open their eyes, and continue by saying, "Everywhere there was light. God made rules for creation: during the day, God told the sun to shine, and at night, he told the beautiful moon and the stars to shine in the night sky."

Let's Learn. In summary, tell the children that God is very wise and loving. He was the one who created the sun with His power.

Activity. Before class-time, cut out the picture of the sun from the worksheet on the following page. You will need one for each child. Instruct the children to color their picture of the sun. Then, help them glue the sun to a tongue depressor or popsicle stick, or something similar.

Conclusion. Pray with the children, thanking God for the sun that warms us and makes the plants grow.

GOD MADE THE SUN

Instructions
Color the picture of the sun, and glue it onto a stick.

LESSON 5: GOD MADE THE MOON

Biblical Basis:
Genesis 1:14-19

Objective:
To know that God created the moon, which lights up the night.

Class Preparation:
Teachers should meet beforehand to pray for the Class Preparation time. Then they should carefully read and reflect on the verses listed under the Biblical Basis.

Introduction

Think about the following:

- The moon, a precious gift from God, is a satellite of earth.
- The moon takes 27 average solar days, seven hours, 43 minutes and 11.6 seconds to go around the earth. This is called a sidereal revolution.
- The synodic revolution of the moon is the time it takes for the moon to return to the same relative position with respect to the sun and the earth. The time of this synodic revolution is approximately 29 days, 12 hours, 44 minutes, and almost three seconds.
- During its movement around the earth, the moon constantly receives sunlight but its angle changes, which is why we see different parts lit up at night. This is called the phases of the moon.

Reflection

According to many sources of information and to the Word of God, there have always been people who have worshiped the sun, the moon, and the stars instead of worshiping the Creator.

In some parts of the world, people still hold on to these beliefs and worship wrongfully.

Thank God that we're more and more committed to serving and pleasing our Creator for all that he has done in our lives.

Let's pray for the salvation of the children in our class and for their parents. Pray that they'll come to know the Creator of all. Let's worship God for being our Creator!

At the end of your prep time together, prepare the materials for your upcoming class.

IMPORTANT INFORMATION:

THEME: GOD MADE THE MOON
BIBLE SCRIPTURE: Genesis 1:14-19

CLASS DEVELOPMENT:

Receive the boys and girls, taking their ages into account. Babies should be placed in cribs, playpens, on blankets or mats — depending on the classroom conditions. Then, welcome all the boys and girls, and indicate where the areas of play and other activities are (this is only for infants from 18 months). In this way, you can make sure that they'll be able to access the previously arranged material in an environment and at a suitable height for their age. This will also allow them to be able to share with their friends and teachers.

At the end of the play/activity time, gather all the children together, making a circle to pray and sing some songs to God, thus starting the lesson of the day.

Let's Talk. Show the children a picture of creation (we will use this picture to show the children the progression of how God created the world). Then, place a picture of the moon below the picture of creation and look at it carefully so that the children will do the same. Then ask, "What are we looking at in this picture?" (Listen to the children's responses.) Then ask, "Have you seen the moon? You can see the moon at night. Have you seen the stars? You can also see the stars at night. Who made the moon? Who made the stars? God made everything. God is so good!"

Let's Play. Now, you can use the picture of creation and glue on the different elements of creation from the first day to now, the creation of the moon. The purpose is to explain what God created by recounting what the students have already been taught. As you add the different elements, discuss the following with your students, "Why did God create this (point to an element of creation on the picture)?" Continue as you discuss each element. End with the moon and explain that they may not see the moon because it comes out at night when they are already asleep. Sing a song that is about the moon.

Next, tell all the children that we're going to pretend to go to sleep (have them lie on the carpet or blankets). Then sing a praise song and explain that this is how many parents and/or family members sing their children to sleep.

Let's Learn. Tell the children that God is very wise and good. He created the moon with his mighty power.

Activity. Provide each child with a worksheet. Help the children trace along the dotted lines of the moon. Then have them color it. Ask them to color the circles that represent the craters with a black or dark color.

Conclusion. Pray to God thanking him for the moon and the stars that give us light at night.

GOD MADE THE MOON

Instructions
Trace along the dotted line; then color the moon. Finish by coloring the small circles black.

LESSON 6

GOD MADE THE FISH

Biblical Basis:
Genesis 1:20-23

Class Preparation:
Teachers should meet beforehand to pray for the Class Preparation time. Then they should carefully read and reflect on the verses listed under the Biblical Basis.

Objective:
To know that God made the fish.

Introduction

Carefully observe the following:

What does the Bible Basis tell us?

Animals and all that God has created are under his rule. Only the power of his Word could create the great giants of the sea, and everything in the sea exists and serves to complement ecology and meet the needs of humans.

For all the beauty that God made, we must be grateful and worship him only.

The species that God has created are diverse: large numbers of fish, mammals, reptiles, amphibians, etc. Fish are aquatic, but so are some mammals; that is to say that their lives unfold underwater and they feel safe there, even reproducing there. Fish are oviparous, that is, they reproduce by laying eggs, whereas mammals are viviparous because their babies are born alive.

Reflection

God wants us to enjoy the beauty of his creation. Therefore, let's be eternally grateful for all he has created. Even the waves of the seas in the thickness of their undulating foam seem to worship God and carry the imperishable memory of the Creator's work.

Let's pray with gratitude for all the beautiful things he has made, and let's recognize that He is our only maker. Let's also pray for the boys and girls in our class and for their parents so that together we can be pleasing to the Lord.

At the end of your preparation time, prepare the fish worksheets and the materials each student will need for the class.

IMPORTANT INFORMATION:

THEME: GOD MADE THE FISH
BIBLE SCRIPTURE: Genesis 1:20-23

CLASS DEVELOPMENT:

Receive the boys and girls, taking their ages into account. Babies should be placed in cribs, playpens, on blankets or mats — depending on the classroom conditions. Then, welcome all the boys and girls, and indicate where the areas of play and other activities are (this is only for infants from 18 months). In this way, you can make sure that they'll be able to access the previously arranged material in an environment and at a suitable height for their age. This will also allow them to be able to share with their friends and teachers.

At the end of the play/activity time, gather all the children together, making a circle to pray and sing some songs to God, thus starting the lesson of the day.

Let's Talk. Provide the children with a picture of creation. (You can continue using the picture from your previous class.) Then, show the children pictures of large and small fish; be sure to include fish that have bright, showy colors. Then ask, "What colors are the fish? Are they all the same size? Who made the fish? Where do they live? What do they eat? How do they swim?"

Finish by reminding the children that God is good and that he made everything beautiful.

Let's Play. Start by gluing fish on the creation picture to include today's lesson. As you do so, review what God created on the first day up to today's class. You can point out the sun, the moon, the stars, the trees, the flowers, the water, the fish; be sure to show the children the aquatic animals of all colors and sizes that swim in the water.

Let's Learn. Tell your little ones that God is good and that he made everything beautiful.

Activity. Give each student a copy of the worksheet. Instruct the children to trace along the dotted lines in the fish picture to make the waves. Then help them use water color paints to paint the fish using cotton swabs as brushes.

Conclusion. End your time together by thanking God for the time to be together and for the opportunity to learn more about him.

GOD MADE THE FISH

Instructions
Trace along the dotted lines to make the waves of the sea; then with a cotton swab, paint the fish.

LESSON 7: GOD MADE THE BIRDS

Biblical Basis:
Genesis 1:20-23

Objective:
To know that God created the birds and be grateful.

Class Preparation:
Teachers should meet beforehand to pray for the Class Preparation time. Then they should carefully read and meditate on the verses listed under the Biblical Basis.

Introduction

Observe and think about the following:

What did God create on the fifth day?

According to the Bible, God commanded, "Let the water teem with living creatures, and let birds fly above the earth across the vault of the sky."

All marine species were created by God, from the great giants to the tiny animals that move in the water.

Birds, which are winged and oviparous, were also created with just the right conditions to reproduce and be part of the divine wealth of God's creation, as well as to be beneficial to human nutritional needs.

God sustains the birds and cares for the lives of these wonderful animals.

There are millions of species of birds in our world.

At the time of the flood, Noah sent a raven to see if the waters had dried up (Genesis 8:7).

Reflection

God, our Creator, is wise and perfect.

We must be thankful to the Lord for everything he has created and treat animals well, for they all represent divine greatness and creation.

Thank God for this wonderful time of meditating on his Word about what he created. Let's not forget to pray for the children in our class and their parents.

At the end of your prayer time, prepare a cardboard bird and two eggs with white paper.

IMPORTANT INFORMATION:

THEME: GOD MADE THE BIRDS
BIBLE SCRIPTURE: Genesis 1:20-23

CLASS DEVELOPMENT:

Receive the boys and girls, taking their ages into account. Babies should be placed in cribs, playpens, on blankets or mats — depending on the classroom conditions. Then, welcome all the boys and girls, and indicate where the areas of play and other activities are (this is only for infants from 18 months). In this way, you can make sure that they'll be able to access the previously arranged material in an environment and at a suitable height for their age. This will also allow them to be able to share with their friends and teachers.

At the end of the play/activity time, gather all the children together, making a circle to pray and sing some songs to God, thus starting the lesson of the day.

Let's Talk. Show the cardboard bird and the two little eggs, or a picture of a hen laying her eggs (mimic the sound a hen makes and encourage the children to also make the sound). Then, tell the children that the hen sits on the eggs all day and all night to keep them warm ... until the chick that is fully formed inside the egg begins to peck at the shell. The chick will continue to peck at the shell until it makes a hole and breaks the shell so it can hatch from the egg. (Here we suggest that you show the children a picture of a chick hatching. Point out the chick's beak and explain how it's made to break the shell.) Then, explain and point out to them on the picture the head, body, and tail. God made the birds.

Let's Play. Paste pictures of birds in the background of the creation picture and ask the children what they are. Reaffirm the responses of the children that they are birds, and tell them that birds have beaks, wings, and feathers. Also add that there are large and small birds, and that birds also sing and fly. Ask the little ones "How do birds fly?" Congratulate them on their responses and let them all "fly" together like birds around the classroom. (Have them flap their arms up and down as if they had wings.) Play or sing a song about birds as they "fly" (search on YouTube).

Let's Learn. Tell your little ones that God made all the birds, from the smallest to the largest. Invite them all to say together, "God is good!"

Activity. Give each child a worksheet. Instruct the children to glue feathers on the body of the little bird or color the bird.

Conclusion. Pray, thanking God for providing us with animals like little birds.

GOD MADE THE BIRDS

Instructions
Glue feathers on the bird's body or color it.

LESSON 8: GOD MADE THE ANIMALS

Biblical Basis:
Genesis 1:24-25

Objective:
To know that God made animals for companionship and to benefit people.

Class Preparation:
Teachers should meet beforehand to pray for the Class Preparation time. Then they should carefully read and meditate on Genesis 1:24-25.

Introduction

Observe and think about the following:

What does the Biblical Basis tell us?
- It tells us that God created animals of all kinds.

How many kinds of animals are there in the world?
- There are countless animals around the world.

What kinds of animals do these verses in Genesis 1:24-25 detail for us?
- Animals are living things that feel and move on their own impulse. Furthermore, they were created by God with the power of his Word and are under his control.

At this point, play a game with the group of teachers that are meeting together. Each teacher needs to say the name of an animal that is in the Bible. However, they can only say the name of animals who are covered with fur. Take turns until they can't think of any more animals. Then change the characteristic or variety and name only fish with scales, or only birds who can't fly, etc...

Next, talk about how animals communicate with each other, how they move, where they live, and what climate they are from.

Reflection

Everything that God created is excellent.

The animal kingdom is huge and amazing. Each animal, in its respective environment, fulfills its life cycle just like people do.

We must love and respect animals.

Pray, thanking God for his wonderful creation of animals. Pray for your students, that they'll be motivated to care for the animals of the world.

When you're done with prayer, prepare the materials for the next lesson.

IMPORTANT INFORMATION:

THEME: GOD MADE THE ANIMALS
BIBLE SCRIPTURE: Genesis 1:24-25

CLASS DEVELOPMENT:

Receive the boys and girls, taking their ages into account. Babies should be placed in cribs, playpens, on blankets or mats — depending on the classroom conditions. Then, welcome all the boys and girls, and indicate where the areas of play and other activities are (this is only for infants from 18 months). In this way, you can make sure that they'll be able to access the previously arranged material in an environment and at a suitable height for their age. This will also allow them to be able to share with their friends and teachers.

At the end of the play/activity time, gather all the children together, making a circle to pray and sing some songs to God, thus starting the lesson of the day.

Let's Talk. Show your class a picture of a girl accompanied by her puppy, and tell the children the following: "Look, here is Lily. Her parents gave her a puppy, and that's why she is so happy. It's the puppy she always wanted to have. The puppy says: 'Bow, wow, wow,' when she runs; and when she turns to look at Lily, her tail wags."

Tell the children that we're going to help Lily choose a name for her puppy. "What do you think Lily should name her puppy?" (Encourage everyone to participate.)

Then add: "What other kinds of animals do you know about? (Encourage everyone to participate.) There are many different animals, and we must remember that we have to take care of them and not mistreat them. God created them and everything he created is good."

Let's Play. Before class, glue pictures of different animals on a piece of cardboard. Now, show the pictures to your class and tell them to look at the animals and see that some have bodies covered in hair. Others are covered in wool. Some have four legs; others two legs. Some live in the city; others in the country on a farm.

Now, sing the song "Old McDonald Had A Farm" and encourage the children to make the different animal sounds as you sing together. After the song, ask the children if they know any animal sounds that you didn't sing about. (You can search YouTube for recorded versions of the song.)

Let's Learn. Remind the little ones that God made all the animals and that each of us must take care of them. Invite them all to say together, "God is so good!"

Activity. In the week before class, ask parents to send in a photo of their child's pet (if they have one) or a picture of an animal that their little one likes. During class, provide each student with a worksheet. Instruct them to glue the picture of their pet or favorite animal in the frame. If they didn't bring a picture, let them color one of the animals at the bottom of the page. Then cut it out and glue it in the frame. Let them decorate around their picture.

Conclusion. Pray, thanking God for creating such beautiful and amazing animals.

GOD MADE THE ANIMALS

Instructions
Glue the photo of your pet or the picture of the animal you like inside the box, and color the animals below.

WEEK 9

LESSON 9: GOD MADE A MAN

Biblical Basis: Genesis 1:26-28

Objective: To know that God made man in His image and likeness.

Class Preparation: Teachers should meet beforehand to pray for the Class Preparation time. Then they should carefully read and reflect on the verses listed under the Biblical Basis.

Introduction

Consider the following:

What does the Biblical Basis tell us?

How was mankind created?

Why did God say the following: "Let's make mankind in our image, in our likeness"?

God created the world, and everything in it, because of his great love. Here is the account of how God created mankind whom he created in his image and likeness for the glory of his name. And everything in the world was created for mankind.

In Acts 17:24-25, we see that God gave mankind intelligence, sensitivity, creativity, and the ability to communicate with him.

Reflection

Let's thank God for all that he has given us. We should be grateful for his love and sustenance and have fellowship with him. In addition, we seek to improve all areas of our lives.

Let's pray, giving thanks to God because we're important to him and because of the special way he created us. Let's also remember to pray for the children in our class, that they'll learn to give thanks to God at their tender age.

As you finish this time of preparation, prepare the materials for the class.

IMPORTANT INFORMATION:

THEME: GOD MADE A MAN
BIBLE SCRIPTURE: Genesis 1:26-28

CLASS DEVELOPMENT:

Receive the boys and girls, taking their ages into account. Babies should be placed in cribs, playpens, on blankets or mats — depending on the classroom conditions. Then, welcome all the boys and girls, and indicate where the areas of play and other activities are (this is only for infants from 18 months). In this way, you can make sure that they'll be able to access the previously arranged material in an environment and at a suitable height for their age. This will also allow them to be able to share with their friends and teachers.

At the end of the play/activity time, gather all the children together, making a circle to pray and sing some songs to God, thus starting the lesson of the day.

Let's Talk. To begin "Let's Talk," ask these amusingly obvious questions to your children: "Has everyone brought their hands? Have you brought your legs? Have you brought your heads?" (Wait for responses from the little ones, then continue.) "That's great! Everyone has brought their hands, their legs, their heads ... Good! So we can all move. Let's sing the song 'Head, shoulders, knees, and toes.'" (You can find this song on YouTube by HeyKids.)

Now, point out and name the different parts of the body, and with the help of the children, say what each of those parts is for. Tell the children that God was very pleased with everything that he made, especially with the man. God made everything, but his work was not complete until he made a man to take care of everything else he had created.

Let's Play. Glue a picture of a man onto the picture of creation that you've been adding to each week. Say, "God made the first man and called him Adam. God gave Adam the responsibility to take care of everything he had created. God gave us hands so we can carry things and work, eyes so we can see, a mouth so we can eat and speak, ears so we can hear, a nose so we can smell, and legs so we can walk, run, and jump everywhere."

Let's Learn. Tell the children that God made man and he was very happy, because everything God made is good.

Activity. Provide a worksheet for each child. Help the children complete the picture by drawing Adam's face. Then, instruct the children to color the rest of the picture.

Conclusion. Pray with the children and then dismiss them, reminding them that they should always be grateful to God because he created us and loves us.

GOD MADE A MAN

Instructions
Draw Adam's face to complete the picture and then color the picture.

LESSON 10 — GOD MADE A WOMAN

Biblical Basis:
Genesis 2:18-25

Class Preparation:
Teachers should meet beforehand to pray for the Class Preparation time. Then they should carefully read and reflect on the verses listed under the Biblical Basis.

Objective:
To know that God made a woman to be a helpmate to man.

Introduction

Think about the following:

What does Genesis 2:18 tell us?

God wasn't finished working yet because he saw that it wasn't good for man to be alone. God didn't create anything bad; on the contrary, "He made everything beautiful" and that is why he was happy. So the man would not be alone, in verses 21 to 23, God made the woman, because both sexes need each other. Thus, the woman was a companion to the man.

The Bible tells us that God placed the man in the garden to work it and take care of it. That was when man was alone. But after a while, God saw that it was not good for man to be alone, so he made the woman.

Reflection

Both man and woman were created in the image and likeness of God. Adam needed someone as a companion, so God created the woman. And it is a great blessing for a man to find a wife (Proverbs 18:22).

Ask the teachers to pray for the great blessing of being created in God's image, and ask him to help you better serve him every day and be a blessing to your students.

As you end your time together, prepare the materials for the class.

IMPORTANT INFORMATION:

THEME: GOD MADE A WOMAN
BIBLE SCRIPTURE: Genesis 2:18-25

CLASS DEVELOPMENT:

Receive the boys and girls, taking their ages into account. Babies should be placed in cribs, playpens, on blankets or mats — depending on the classroom conditions. Then, welcome all the boys and girls, and indicate where the areas of play and other activities are (this is only for infants from 18 months). In this way, you can make sure that they'll be able to access the previously arranged material in an environment and at a suitable height for their age. This will also allow them to be able to share with their friends and teachers.

At the end of the play/activity time, gather all the children together, making a circle to pray and sing some songs to God, thus starting the lesson of the day.

Let's Talk. Show the children the picture of creation you've added to each week and talk about the following: "Do you remember all the things that God made?… (Wait for their responses, then continue.) He made the trees, the flowers, the fruit, the sun, the moon, the stars, the animals, the man … And what else did he make?" (Wait for the answers from the little ones.) "He also made a woman; he made her from Adam's rib and called her Eve." (Now, glue a picture of a woman next to Adam on the creation picture.) God created the woman with hands, legs, a head, a body, a heart, etc… just like the man. And when God had finished making her, he placed her next to Adam; and when Adam saw her, he was very happy."

Let's Play. Have the children stand in a circle, and ask them to move their body and point to different body parts, repeating the name of each part. Then each teacher should point to a part of their body and encourage the children to say out loud what it is. Then, sing "My Body" by ABC mouse.com (found on YouTube) or a similar song about the body.

Let's Learn. Remind your little ones that everything God does is good.

Activity. Provide a worksheet for each child. Have the children color the picture of the woman and then help them glue wool (yarn) on the picture as the woman's hair.

Conclusion. Spend time in prayer, thanking God for creating Eve and other women. Continue by thanking God for the different women in our lives, like our moms, grandmothers, teachers, etc…

GOD MADE A WOMAN

Instructions

Color the picture. Then glue yarn on the picture to make the woman's hair.

33

LESSON 11: THANK YOU, GOD, FOR DADDY AND MOMMY

Biblical Basis: Exodus 20:12

Objective: To know that God made daddy and mommy and be thankful for them.

Class Preparation: Teachers should meet beforehand to pray for the Class Preparation time. Then they should carefully read and meditate on the verses listed under the Biblical Basis.

Introduction

Despite sad family stories, and how badly some parents treat their children, it is necessary to talk to our children about the importance of obeying parents. Our task, as teachers, is to teach families about the light of the Word of God, teaching the importance of obeying God's command to honor our parents from an early age. Many of our children may only hear this in church. Prepare yourself to teach this much needed theme but not without stopping to consider that it's also possible that some of your small students come from difficult situations. You may have children who have been orphaned, abandoned by one or both parents, or live in other difficult situations. Ask God for discernment and wisdom to share the love of God with these little ones who are in your care.

Reflection

How important we all are to God! Both men and women.

For the Lord, there is no significance of persons. We're all unique and valuable to him.

God cares about us and helps us to be fulfilled in our marriages.

He blesses our marriages from the beginning if we allow ourselves to be guided by his will.

Spouses should love each other. Wives are to "respect" their husbands and husbands must "love" their wives (Ephesians 5:21-28).

Pray, thanking God for our gender. Also pray for the gender of the children in your class, that they'll develop healthily and within the framework of holiness.

At the end of your prayer time, prepare the materials for your upcoming class.

IMPORTANT INFORMATION:

THEME: THANK YOU, GOD, FOR DADDY AND MOMMY
BIBLE SCRIPTURE: Exodus 20:12

CLASS DEVELOPMENT:

Receive the boys and girls, taking their ages into account. Babies should be placed in cribs, playpens, on blankets or mats — depending on the classroom conditions. Then, welcome all the boys and girls, and indicate where the areas of play and other activities are (this is only for infants from 18 months). In this way, you can make sure that they'll be able to access the previously arranged material in an environment and at a suitable height for their age. This will also allow them to be able to share with their friends and teachers.

At the end of the play/activity time, gather all the children together, making a circle to pray and sing some songs to God, thus starting the lesson of the day.

Let's Talk. Show your class pictures of different kinds of families (Families with two parents, with one parent, with a grandparent(s), etc. (You can cut them out of magazines, newspapers, etc. beforehand.) Ask them to point to a dad, a mom, children, and other family members, if any. Then, ask: "Why do we have families? What do our mommies and daddies do for us?" (Give them time to express their ideas, then continue.) "They take care of us, they feed us, they buy us clothes, etc. Also, it's nice because we can play with our brothers and sisters and our parents, and we can read the Bible and pray together as a family. Our family should always helps us. We're thankful to God for mommy and daddy. The Lord made them because he knew that they were important in our lives. Who gave us our family?" (Answer: God.) "So, since God gave us our family, we know that God loves us very much because of the blessing he has given to us."

Let's Play. Using the pictures you showed the class during the Let's Talk time, play some games with the children that are related to the family. As you finish up play time, sing "O-B-E-Y" with the Donut Man (search on YouTube). You could also teach the children the song "Make Your Dad Glad" with the Donut Man (it talks about family).

Let's Learn. Remind the children that families are a wonderful creation of God.

Activity. Provide a worksheet for each child. Help your little ones draw a circle around the faces of the mommy and daddy. Let them color the picture.

Conclusion. Tell the boys and girls that we must remember that Adam and Eve were the first people that God created. Pray, thanking the Lord that children obey their parents.

THANK YOU, GOD, FOR DADDY AND MOMMY

Always Together

Instructions
Draw a circle around the faces of mommy and daddy, and then color the picture.

LESSON 12
THANK YOU, GOD, FOR COLORS

Biblical Basis:

Genesis 1:31;
Ecclesiastes 3:11-12

Class Preparation:
Teachers should meet beforehand to pray for the Class Preparation time. Then they should carefully read and meditate on the verses listed under the Biblical Basis.

Objective:
To know that everything God made has color and He has given us the ability to see those colors.

Introduction

Read and meditate on the Biblical Basis.

What did God do?

God gave perfect color to his creation. All things have a specific color: the sky, the sea, the sun, plants, flowers, fruits, animals, etc. We human beings, as blessed children, can see everything in its original color. What would it be like if we could only see things in black and white? How would we feel? What if the world had no color?

God made everything, understanding the needs of the world. That includes the beautiful colors and tones that he gave to each thing. God made the rainbow, which consists of seven colors, which was a sign of the promise he made with his creation to never again destroy all life by a flood; it also represents the natural colors and all the wonderful things that only he can make.

Reflection

How beautiful are the colors that God has created!

Besides black and white and the primary colors, God created a large range of colors for us to enjoy.

What are some things that are red? Apple, tomato, strawberry, etc.

What is yellow? The banana, the mango, the sun, etc.

What is blue? The sky, the sea, the river, etc.

Pray, asking the Lord to allow us to perceive things, attitudes, and behaviors as they really are so that we can help our children and their parents.

After prayer, prepare the materials for the class and make a sample of the craft to show the children.

IMPORTANT INFORMATION:

THEME: THANK YOU, GOD, FOR COLORS
BIBLE SCRIPTURES: Genesis 1:31; Ecclesiastes 3:11-12

CLASS DEVELOPMENT:

Receive the boys and girls, taking their ages into account. Babies should be placed in cribs, playpens, on blankets or mats — depending on the classroom conditions. Then, welcome all the boys and girls, and indicate where the areas of play and other activities are (this is only for infants from 18 months). In this way, you can make sure that they'll be able to access the previously arranged material in an environment and at a suitable height for their age. This will also allow them to be able to share with their friends and teachers.

At the end of the play/activity time, gather all the children together, making a circle to pray and sing some songs to God, thus starting the lesson of the day.

Let's Talk. Share with the children that God made the sky, the earth, the sun, the moon, the stars, the animals, the fish, the plants, the man, and the woman, and he created each of them with unique natural color. The Lord has given us the blessing of seeing those natural colors, colors that only he could make: red, blue, green, yellow, etc.

Now, take the children for a short walk around the church building, meeting place, or even outside. Help them observe the environment. Encourage them to see the colors around them and to realize that everything has a color.

At the end of the walk, encourage them to always thank God for everything.

Let's Play. Select several objects of different colors. Tell the children that they can pick up these objects. Then explain to them that when you say a color, you want them to find an object that is the same color. For example, "Pick up something red." (Give the children adequate time so that everyone can find a red object from the objects you've presented them.) We recommended playing this game to help the little ones become familiar with their colors and easily recognize them, especially the basic colors.

Let's Learn. Remind the children that God created colors and he has given us the blessing of being his children.

Activity. Provide a worksheet for each child. Provide the children with green, red, and yellow clay or play-doh or paper and have them glue it onto the rainbow. Then have them glue blue clay or paper onto the clouds.

Conclusion. Pray, thanking God for making the rainbow, which reminds us that He cares for us and loves us.

THANK YOU, GOD, FOR COLORS

Instructions
Glue green, red, and yellow modeling clay or paper on the rainbow and blue modeling clay or paper inside the clouds.

LESSON 13: MY GOD MADE EVERYTHING BEAUTIFUL

Biblical Basis: Psalm 145:1-10

Class Preparation: Teachers should meet beforehand to pray for the Class Preparation time. Then they should carefully read and meditate on the verses listed under the Biblical Basis.

Objective: To know that everything God created is beautiful and meaningful.

Introduction

Reflect on the Biblical Basis.

The psalmist expressed what his heart felt.

We realize that no one can go without noticing and being in awe of what God has created.

How beautiful is everything we see! All of nature that God has created, the things that can be transformed through the wisdom that he has granted to mankind, and the happiness that he gives us when we put all our trust in our Creator.

In Colossians 1:16-17, the apostle Paul revealed that Christ — the only begotten Son of God who came to bring peace to the world — fulfilled the desire of his heavenly Father by participating in the creation of the world; for in Him all things were created. Yes it is true that there are negative or harmful things in the world; however in everything, we're sure that our refuge and comfort is Jehovah our God, and Christ is the head of the church.

Reflection

- God is infinite and unequaled.
- He made everything beautiful and significant.
- God is unchanging.
- Jesus Christ is the Son of God.
- The Holy Spirit guides us and is our Comforter.

Pray for this precious time of preparation and for the commitment to teach God's truth to these young children.

At the end of your prayer time, prepare the materials for the upcoming class.

IMPORTANT INFORMATION:

THEME: MY GOD MADE EVERYTHING BEAUTIFUL
BIBLE SCRIPTURE: Psalm 145:1-10

CLASS DEVELOPMENT:

Receive the boys and girls, taking their ages into account. Babies should be placed in cribs, playpens, on blankets or mats — depending on the classroom conditions. Then, welcome all the boys and girls, and indicate where the areas of play and other activities are (this is only for infants from 18 months). In this way, you can make sure that they'll be able to access the previously arranged material in an environment and at a suitable height for their age. This will also allow them to be able to share with their friends and teachers.

At the end of the play/activity time, gather all the children together, making a circle to pray and sing some songs to God, thus starting the lesson of the day.

Let's Talk. Summarize with the children everything they've previously studied, reminding them that God made all things. Use the creation picture from the previous classes, pointing out the things that God created in the order that they happened. (If you prefer, you can use a new picture for this class.) As you point out the different events, let the children say what they are. For example: sky, earth, sun, moon, stars, animals, fish, plants, man, woman, etc. Encourage all the little ones to participate. When you're done, thank God for everything he created.

Let's Play. Take the children to an area with lots of space or adapt your classroom by moving furniture out of the way. Draw two parallel lines (or use tape). One line represents the "water" and the other line will represent the "land." Then have the children stand next to one of the lines. Tell them that at the signal they are hop, with their feet together, to the line that represents the word you say. So, when you say "water," they hop to that line. When you say "land," they hop to the other line. Everyone should hop carefully, applauding and thanking God for all the beauty he has created.

Let's Learn. Tell the children that God has given us the best and most beautiful gifts because he created them with love.

Activity. Have a worksheet for each child. Ask the little ones to draw a circle around what they like most about God's creation, and then have them color the entire picture.

Conclusion. Pray, thanking God for the time to be together and learn more from Him.

MY GOD MADE EVERYTHING BEAUTIFUL

Instructions
Draw a circle around what you like best about God's creation. Then color the picture.

UNIT 2

KNOWING AND ENJOYING WHAT GOD HAS CREATED

WEEK 1:	DAY AND NIGHT	44
WEEK 2:	GOD PLANTED A BEAUTIFUL GARDEN	47
WEEK 3:	WHAT IS "LIGHT" FOR?	50
WEEK 4:	MY LITTLE LIGHT WILL SHINE	53
WEEK 5:	THERE IS WATER ALL OVER THE WORLD	56
WEEK 6:	I AM THE LIVING WATER	59
WEEK 7:	THE SUN LIGHTS UP THE DAY	62
WEEK 8:	THE MOON LIGHTS UP THE NIGHT	65
WEEK 9:	GOD CREATED THE PRETTY FISH	68
WEEK 10:	THE LITTLE BIRDS SING TO GOD	71
WEEK 11:	ANIMALS ARE VERY IMPORTANT	74
WEEK 12:	BOYS AND GIRLS WERE CREATED BY GOD	77
WEEK 13:	WHAT IS MY FAMILY LIKE?	80

LESSON 14
DAY AND NIGHT

Biblical Basis:
Genesis 1:3-5

Objective:
To know about day and night and thank God for these wonders.

Class Preparation:
Teachers should meet beforehand to pray for the Class Preparation time.

Introduction

Think carefully about the Bible reading from the Biblical Basis.

God created the world with a very wholesome and special purpose. In Genesis chapter 1, we find in the first two verses that the earth was formless and empty. But the power of the voice of the Creator caused the earth itself, and all of heaven, to obey and be placed as it should be.

The Psalmist affirms the following: "For he spoke, and it came to be; he commanded, and it stood firm"(Psalm 33:9). Notice that God called the light "day" and he called the darkness "night." God saw that the light was good and separated it from the darkness; so, day and night became two periods of time to be used for certain activities. For example, day is the time to be active, work, and interact with society, the time of greatest exertion. And night is to rest by sleeping.

Reflection

God knew our need for light and darkness from the beginning; he knew we would need exercise and rest to be healthy. Therefore, day and night are useful and necessary for us. Likewise, we find spiritual light in Christ, because He is the light of the world (John 8:12). Therefore we, the sons and daughters of God, must be light to the world in the midst of the darkness of sin.

Let's pray for this precious time, and for our students and their parents, that all of them will give their lives to Christ our Savior.

At the end of your prayer time, prepare the materials for the lesson.

IMPORTANT INFORMATION:

THEME: DAY AND NIGHT

BIBLE SCRIPTURE: Genesis: 1:3-5

CLASS DEVELOPMENT:

Receive the boys and girls, taking their ages into account. Babies should be placed in cribs, playpens, on blankets or mats — depending on the classroom conditions. Then, welcome all the boys and girls, and indicate where the areas of play and other activities are (this is only for infants from 18 months). In this way, you can make sure that they'll be able to access the previously arranged material in an environment and at a suitable height for their age. This will also allow them to be able to share with their friends and teachers.

At the end of the play/activity time, gather all the children together, making a circle to pray and sing some songs to God, thus starting the lesson of the day.

Let's Talk. Show the children a colorful picture of a boy or girl sleeping in their bed, and discuss the following: "What is the boy (or girl) doing? When do we sleep? Why do we sleep at night? Why don't we sleep during the day? What do we do during the day?" (Wait for the children to respond and encourage everyone to participate, then continue.) "Let's remember that the night is dark and the moon shines in the sky, while the day is bright. So, the day is light, it is clear, so we can run, jump, play, or walk with mommy and daddy."

Finish this section by reminding children that God made all things.

Let's Play. Place the children in a circle and give each of them a paper telescope. (Make these ahead of time out of toilet paper rolls or cardboard tubes. Decorate them with paper and have one end covered with a removable cover. See ideas on the Internet.) First, hand them the telescopes with the lens covered, and ask them to look in them. Ask them if they can see anything. Tell them that this is called darkness, and it is similar to night. Then, take the cover off of the telescopes and have them to look again. Ask them if they can see anything. Tell them that light is related to day. Pray thanking God for day and night.

Let's Learn. Tell the boys and girls that God made the light and the darkness, day and night, and because of all that God has created, we enjoy everything beautiful.

Activity. Provide a worksheet for each child. Instruct the children to complete the face pictures (one should be awake and one asleep) and color them.

Conclusion. Pray, thanking God for all the beauty he has created, for the time to be together and for being able to learn more about him.

DAY AND NIGHT

Instructions

Draw the face of a person who is awake and another that is asleep. Then color the picture.

LESSON 15: GOD PLANTED A BEAUTIFUL GARDEN

Biblical Basis:
Genesis 2:8-14

Objective:
To know that God gave people a beautiful place to live happily.

Class Preparation:
Teachers should meet beforehand to pray for the Class Preparation time. Then they should carefully read and meditate on the verses listed under the Biblical Basis.

Introduction

Let's carefully note the following:

What does the word "Eden" mean? What was Eden?

Why did God create this garden?

Who did God put in Eden?

What did God put in the middle of the garden? What came out of Eden?

Eden means "delightful region; paradise or a state of perfect happiness." In Eden, God planted, among other things, the tree of life and the tree of the knowledge of good and evil.

The word "paradise" is synonymous with "heaven, as the final abode of the righteous."

Because of the love that God has for man, he placed this very special creation in a very beautiful place that not only had plants, animals, hills, and mountains but the beauty was completed by a fresh and mighty river that watered the garden. Man would be the administrator of all God created; that was God's intention. For this reason, he made an ideal helper and companion for man: a woman, taken from the rib of the man. God's Word tells us this in Genesis 2:22. God reveals his love for us in all that he has created for us to enjoy.

Reflection

God, as the Author of life, has always known the needs of people.

The garden signifies the beautiful and meaningful things that God gives to man and woman.

We must remember that we're only stewards of the things that God gives us.

Let's take care of the environment and everything that God has created.

Let's pray, thanking God for his amazing love and for creation. Pray for the children in your class and their parents; he has made us all and we're all his very blessed creatures.

As you finish this time together, prepare the materials for the class.

IMPORTANT INFORMATION:

THEME: GOD PLANTED A BEAUTIFUL GARDEN
BIBLE SCRIPTURE: Genesis 2:8-14

CLASS DEVELOPMENT:

Receive the boys and girls, taking their ages into account. Babies should be placed in cribs, playpens, on blankets or mats — depending on the classroom conditions. Then, welcome all the boys and girls, and indicate where the areas of play and other activities are (this is only for infants from 18 months). In this way, you can make sure that they'll be able to access the previously arranged material in an environment and at a suitable height for their age. This will also allow them to be able to share with their friends and teachers.

At the end of the play/activity time, gather all the children together, making a circle to pray and sing some songs to God, thus starting the lesson of the day.

Let's Talk. Prepare ahead of time to have a large picture of creation with all its elements to show the class. Make sure it is large enough that all the students can easily see it.

Have the children look at the picture and talk about what God created. (Give them time to look at everything and name the colors, sizes, and location of various elements. For example: the sun is yellow and is in the sky, the fish is blue and lives in the sea, etc...) Then, show them that each created thing is good for something. God placed each thing in the best place. He knew where it was needed. We know that everything God created is beautiful, that everything has a place, that everything is good for something, and that everything has color, and all that God created is good. All this was possible because God created everything in his wisdom.

Let's Play. Before class, set out around the classroom different things created by God (for example: an apple, a flower, etc...). Include some things that were created by people as a complement to the wisdom that God has given us. (For example: a wheel, a light bulb, etc...) Ask the children to look carefully at the items and talk about whether they're man made or created by God. Then, sing a song about God creating the world. Creation Song, by Early Childhood Worship by Saddleback Kids, is a good one. (Search YouTube for this song or others.) Make sure you use actions when you sing the song.

Let's Learn. Remind the children that God made a beautiful world for all of us to enjoy.

Activity. Provide a worksheet for each child. Tell the children to color the picture using lots of different colored crayons or pencils.

Conclusion. Pray, thanking God for all that he created. And say together with all the children, "Thank You, God, for all that You created!"

GOD PLANTED A BEAUTIFUL GARDEN

Instructions
Color the picture using lots of different colors.

LESSON 16: WHAT IS "LIGHT" FOR?

 Biblical Basis:
Genesis 1:3-4 and 1:14-19

 Objective:
To know that God made the sun, the moon and the stars to give light to the earth.

 Class Preparation
Teachers should meet beforehand to pray for the Class Preparation time. Then they should carefully read and meditate on Genesis 1:3-4, 14-19.

Introduction

Let's carefully note the following:

What does the Word of God tell us in Genesis 1:3-4 and 1:14-19?

Why did God make the "lights in the sky"?

Why do we think these wonders were created on the fourth day?

What is the function of "lights" in our world?

In Genesis 1:3-4, we see that God created the light on the first day and after making it, he saw that it was good. Then he separated the light from the darkness. And he gave them their respective names: day and night.

Light is essential for life itself. Light guides us and gives us illumination when we need it.

Light allows us to see things clearly, just as they are.

In Psalm 27:1, David emphatically said, "The Lord is my light and my salvation …". King David recognized that God was the only one who could illuminate his life and who can safely lead us in the midst of a world of darkness.

Reflection

The first thing God did was to give light to the world, and he gives light to our lives.

Light is a symbol of salvation.

Christians give light to the world by sharing their testimony of what God has done in their lives.

Jesus is the light of the world.

Pray that the light of Christ will shine in the hearts of our children and in their parents so they'll come to the feet of Jesus.

At the end of your prayer time, prepare the materials for upcoming lesson.

IMPORTANT INFORMATION:

THEME: WHAT IS "LIGHT" FOR?
BIBLE SCRIPTURE: Genesis: 1:3-4, 14-19

CLASS DEVELOPMENT:

Receive the boys and girls, taking their ages into account. Babies should be placed in cribs, playpens, on blankets or mats — depending on the classroom conditions. Then, welcome all the boys and girls, and indicate where the areas of play and other activities are (this is only for infants from 18 months). In this way, you can make sure that they'll be able to access the previously arranged material in an environment and at a suitable height for their age. This will also allow them to be able to share with their friends and teachers.

At the end of the play/activity time, gather all the children together, making a circle to pray and sing some songs to God, thus starting the lesson of the day.

Let's Talk. Show the picture of the creation from you previous classes, and ask the children to point to the sun, moon, and stars. Then ask them: "What are the sun, moon and stars for? When does the sun rise? When does the moon rise? When do we see the stars?" (Wait and encourage everyone to participate, then continue.) "They all give us light, just as God created them to. God is so good! The sun makes the day more beautiful, and the moon and the stars shine in the darkness of the night."

Let's Play. Take the children for a walk outside. Have them hold hands and stay together. When you get outside, ask them to show you where the sun is and then show them where the moon and stars can be seen at night.

Let's Learn. Tell the little ones that God made the light so that we can all have light.

Activity. Provide each student with a worksheet. Instruct the children to trace along the dotted line to form the star and then to color it. Help them cut it out. Then, give them a piece of heavy black paper or cardstock that is just a little bigger than the star and help them glue their star on the paper, and then on the opposite side, glue the verse.

Conclusion. Pray with the children, thanking God for everything in creation that he made. As you finish the prayer, tell the children to say all together, "Thank you, God, for light."

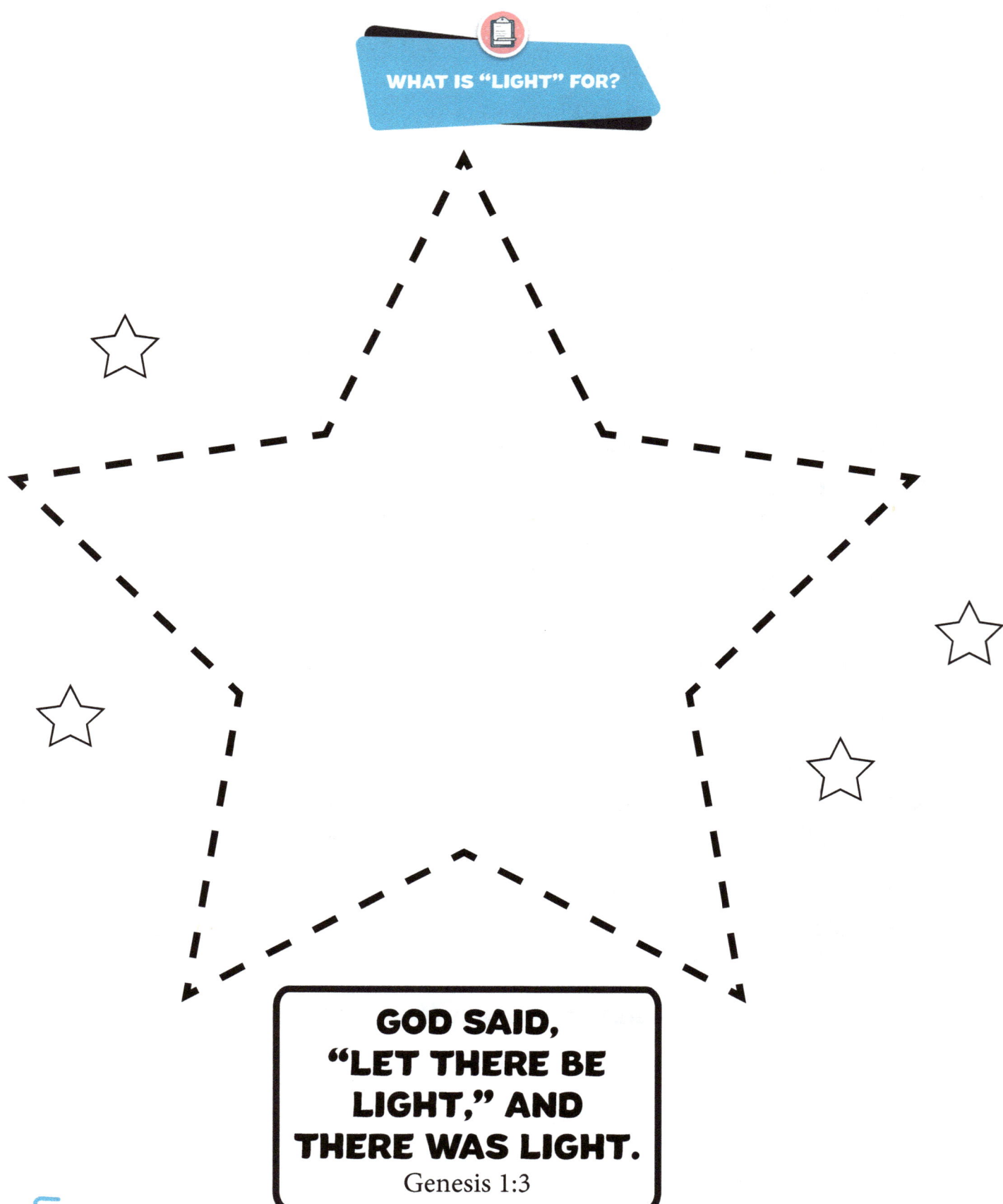

LESSON 17: MY LITTLE LIGHT WILL SHINE

Biblical Basis:
Matthew 5:14-16, 1 John 1:7

Class Preparation:
Teachers should meet beforehand to pray for the Class Preparation time. Then they should carefully read and meditate on the verses listed under the Biblical Basis.

Objective:
To know that their light can guide other children to Jesus.

Introduction

Let's carefully consider the following:

What does the apostle John tell us in 1 John 1:7?

How should we walk?

Who gave us the example of walking in the light?

What will our life be like when we walk in the light?

According to Matthew 5:14, what does Jesus tell us we are?

According to Matthew 5:16, how should we present our light?

Ever since the time of Christ, the Bible and Christ's church have written about and recommended that we should walk in the light, as a way to proclaim we're Christians.

Jesus Himself was an example of being a guide and shining light in the darkness of sin where the great majority of people walk.

Our light should serve as a guide to light up the path for others to find Jesus Christ.

Reflection

The Lord has called us to be "light" in the midst of a world of darkness, to bring others into the light of Christ.

Every life that has received Christ is a light that reflects the love and grace of Christ.

Boys and girls, from early childhood, can allow their little lights to shine through their lifestyle, through their conduct, and through their knowledge of Jesus.

As you end the time of preparation, prepare the materials for the upcoming lesson.

IMPORTANT INFORMATION:

THEME: MY LITTLE LIGHT WILL SHINE
BIBLE SCRIPTURES: Matthew 5:14-16; 1 John 1:7

CLASS DEVELOPMENT:

Receive the boys and girls, taking their ages into account. Babies should be placed in cribs, playpens, on blankets or mats — depending on the classroom conditions. Then, welcome all the boys and girls, and indicate where the areas of play and other activities are (this is only for infants from 18 months). In this way, you can make sure that they'll be able to access the previously arranged material in an environment and at a suitable height for their age. This will also allow them to be able to share with their friends and teachers.

At the end of the play/activity time, gather all the children together, making a circle to pray and sing some songs to God, thus starting the lesson of the day.

Let's Talk. Begin by reviewing the previous theme, talking with the children about the following: "What lights up our days? Yes, the sun. What shines on us at night? Correct, the moon. What else shines on us at night? Yes, the stars. What do all of these provide for us? Light! The light from the sun, moon, and stars provides light for us. And children, can we shine? Can we be light to others? Yes, we can. By being good children and by inviting our friends to church, we can be a light to guide others to Jesus."

Let's Play. Gather the children inside the classroom and close the door carefully. Then, give each child a flashlight that is turned on and line them up. Sing the song, "This Little Light of Mine." Then, thank God for allowing us to carry the light of his Word to our family and friends.

Let's Learn. Tell the children that God has created each one of us and has put us in this world to be lights. We can be a light that will guide our friends and our family to know and follow Jesus.

Activity. Provide a worksheet for each child. Instruct the children to draw along the dotted line with a blue marker or crayon. Then have them decorate it however they'd like.

Conclusion. Thank God for letting us carry the light of his Word to our world.

MY LITTLE LIGHT WILL SHINE

Instructions
Draw along the dotted lines with a blue marker or crayon. Then decorate the picture however you'd like.

LESSON 18: THERE IS WATER ALL OVER THE WORLD

Biblical Basis:
Genesis 1:6-8;
Psalm 23:2, 114:8

Objective:
To know that everything God has created is useful in our lives and the lives of others.

Class Preparation:
Teachers should meet beforehand to pray for the Class Preparation time. Then they should carefully read and meditate on the verses listed under the Biblical Basis.

Introduction

Think carefully about the following:

What do the verses of the Biblical Basis tell us?

What is the importance of water?

Why did God consider it vital for creation?

In the Bible, we find water is used as an expression of joy and peace for the life of the afflicted and an element for people to experience God's care (Psalm 23:2).

However, in the Bible water also represents distress and fear. But God shows his love to us by offering his help to us when we're afraid and in times of trial (Isaiah 43:2).

In the New Testament, Jesus teaches us through the parable of "The Rich Man and Lazarus" that in desperation, the rich man recognized that water would cool his tongue in the torment of the fire (Luke 16:24).

Jesus Christ, the Son of God, is the living water. We learn this from Jesus' conversation with the Samaritan woman when he offered her the living water, the same living water that he offers to each of us.

Rivers, seas, lakes, streams, etc. are all made of the liquid called water, which is a necessity that God's creatures can't live without.

Reflection

God, in his infinite wisdom, created everything that is indispensable.

Because God loves people, he created water as an indispensable element for life.

Children must be taught to take care of our water sources and to help keep our environment clean.

Let's pray, thanking God for water that meets our physical needs, and thank God for giving us the living water which satisfies our spiritual thirst through his beloved Son, Jesus Christ.

At the end of your time together, prepare the materials for the class.

IMPORTANT INFORMATION:

THEME: THERE IS WATER ALL OVER THE WORLD
BIBLE SCRIPTURES: Genesis 1:6-8; Psalm 23:2, 114:8

CLASS DEVELOPMENT:

Receive the boys and girls, taking their ages into account. Babies should be placed in cribs, playpens, on blankets or mats — depending on the classroom conditions. Then, welcome all the boys and girls, and indicate where the areas of play and other activities are (this is only for infants from 18 months). In this way, you can make sure that they'll be able to access the previously arranged material in an environment and at a suitable height for their age. This will also allow them to be able to share with their friends and teachers.

At the end of the play/activity time, gather all the children together, making a circle to pray and sing some songs to God, thus starting the lesson of the day.

Let's Talk. Review with the children what you talked about in the last class. Include the following: "Who remembers what we talked about last week?" (Wait and encourage everyone to participate, then continue.) "Very good! We talked about light, but God also made water. In the beginning, there was lots of water in the world. Then, God separated the waters, and the sky appeared above and water below. That was beautiful! Now, we have water to bathe in, to play in, to use to clean up and for mom to use to prepare food. We also get water from the rain that refreshes the environment, which is another way God blesses us with water."

Let's Play. Have the boys and girls wash their hands and faces using a large bowl for water and soap. Be prepared with a towel or paper towels, a comb, and a mirror so that they can also comb their hair (or have their hair combed by a teacher). Then talk to the children about the importance for personal hygiene and how we use water to keep ourselves clean.

Let's Learn. Explain to the children that God has created water in large quantities that we find in rivers, lakes, and seas. He has created water for us so we need to thank him for it.

Activity. Provide a worksheet for each child. Give each child cotton to glue on their picture to fill in the clouds. Then, instruct the children to trace along the dotted lines using a thick light blue marker.

Conclusion. Ask the children to sit in a circle and put their hands together to thank God for providing lots of water in the world.

THERE IS WATER ALL OVER THE WORLD

Instructions

Glue cotton to make the clouds. Trace along the dotted lines with a thick light blue marker.

LESSON 19: I AM THE LIVING WATER

Biblical Basis:
Revelation 7:16-17, 21:6
John 7:38

Objective:
For the children to know that they are a source of blessing to their families and others.

Class Preparation:
Teachers should meet beforehand to pray for the Class Preparation time. Then carefully read the verses listed under the Biblical Basis.

Introduction

Let's think carefully about the content of the Biblical Basis reading.

What did Jesus Christ mean when he referred to living water flowing from believers?

What is the meaning of water in each of the verses you've read?

What happens to the one who believes in Christ?

According to Revelation 21:6, what should we do when we're thirsty? What was the revelation given to the Apostle John? Who is the Alpha and the Omega?

According to Revelation 7:17, where will the Lamb of God lead us?

At the Feast of Tabernacles, Jesus was motivated to declare to the world that the water that he offered was completely free and that those who put all their trust in God could obtain it immediately.

Peace and well-being are compared to the water of the river and the waves of the sea; this is if we pay attention to the commandments of our God (Isaiah 48:18).

Water is very necessary and useful. It has been scientifically proven to consist of two parts hydrogen and one part oxygen (H_2O). It solidifies at 0° C and boils at 100° C.

Reflection

The wisdom and love that God has shown us from the beginning of creation should make us feel very confident.

Water, both in the world and in the body of the human being, is found in large quantities, thus contributing to the well-being of life.

The freshness and spiritual vitality that the Christian fosters and imparts to the unbelieving world is the blessing that God has left us to take advantage of by carrying his Word every day, because rivers of living water now flow from within us.

Let's pray for the children and their parents and also for the life of each one of the teachers that they'll be good examples of Christians.

At the end of your prayer time, prepare the materials for the lesson.

IMPORTANT INFORMATION:

THEME: I AM THE LIVING WATER

BIBLE SCRIPTURES: John 7:38; Revelation 7:16-17, 21:6

CLASS DEVELOPMENT:

Receive the boys and girls, taking their ages into account. Babies should be placed in cribs, playpens, on blankets or mats — depending on the classroom conditions. Then, welcome all the boys and girls, and indicate where the areas of play and other activities are (this is only for infants from 18 months). In this way, you can make sure that they'll be able to access the previously arranged material in an environment and at a suitable height for their age. This will also allow them to be able to share with their friends and teachers.

At the end of the play/activity time, gather all the children together, making a circle to pray and sing some songs to God, thus starting the lesson of the day.

Let's Talk. Show the boys and girls the picture of the landscape of creation and point out the rivers and the sea. Ask each of them to repeat the word "river." Then remind them that God created the rivers — when a river is still, it is a symbol of peace. Jesus tells us that whoever believes in him will have life and peace.

Let's Play. Before class time, make wavy lines on the floor with tape or something that is removable. When it's time for "Let's Play," instruct the children to walk along the wavy lines, trying to stay on the line. Have them first walk with their little hands at their side, and then have them carrying small bags of cookies on their heads.

Let's Learn. Emphasize that God has created rivers and gives us the opportunity to have abundant peace if we ask in faith.

Activity. Ask parents to send a t-shirt with their child to class. The shirt is for their little ones to use to protect their nice clothes. The t-shirt can be used, or the teacher can provide a t-shirt or aprons for each child. During class, give each student a worksheet. Then, give them light blue paint and a paint brush and help them paint the river.

Conclusion. Pray giving thanks to God because we can trust him at all times, and we all can share his Word.

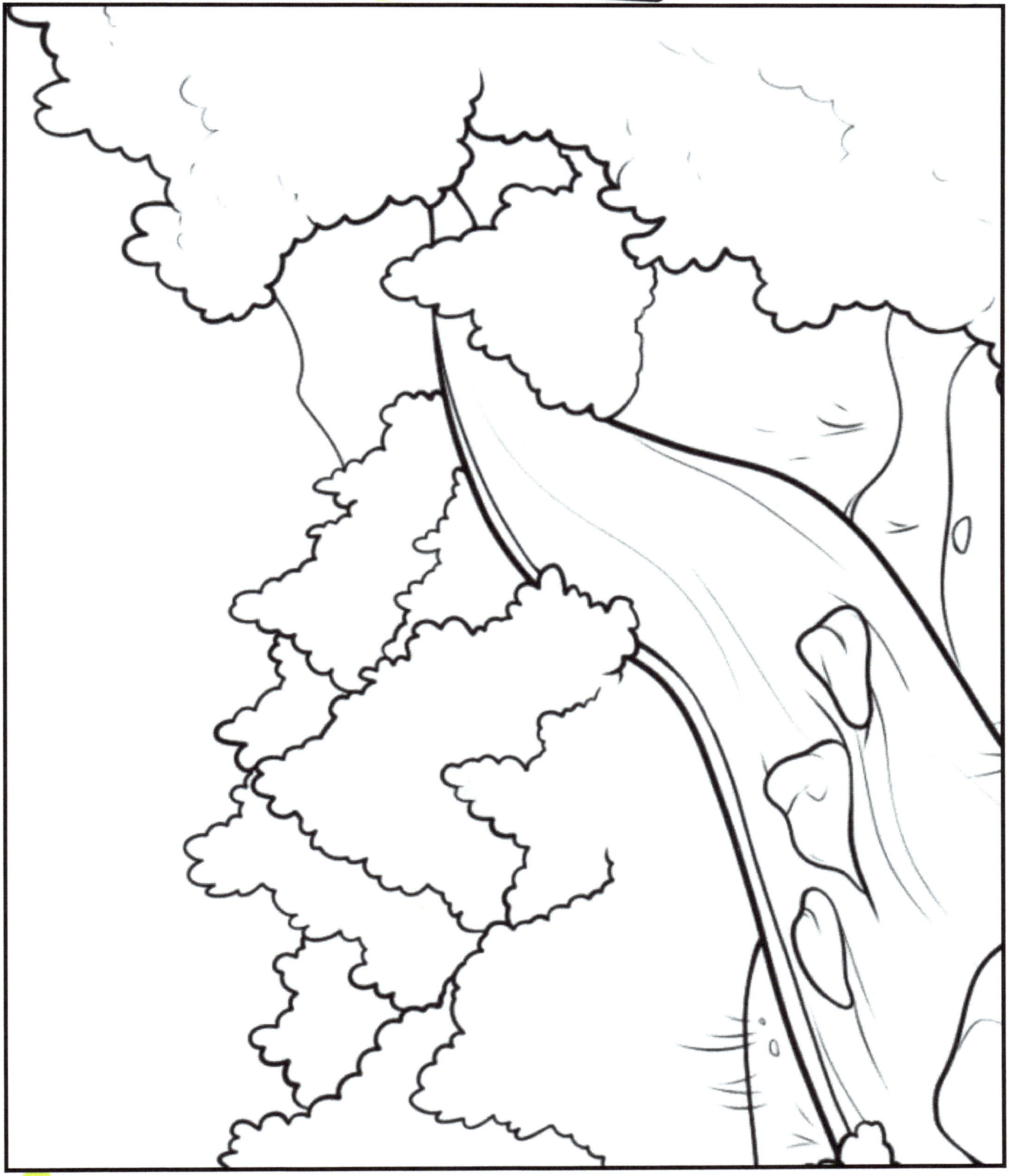

I AM THE LIVING WATER

Instructions
Paint the river with light blue paint, using a cotton swab.

LESSON 20: THE SUN LIGHTS UP THE DAY

Biblical Basis:
Genesis 1:14-19

Objective:
To know that God made the sun as the major light source to light up our days.

Class Preparation:
Teachers should meet beforehand to pray for the Class Preparation time. Then meditate on the verses listed under the Biblical Basis.

Introduction

Let's think carefully about the following:

What is the function of the two great lights that God created?

What other role do these lights play?

Where did God put these great lights?

What other lights did God make?

The Word of God teaches us that in the beginning, there was only darkness and disorder. God's plan was always to provide the best for humanity; therefore, the light or clarity that the sun provides us also generates order in the world. It was positioned to establish day and night, and it affects the change of seasons, the climate and temperature, as well as the advancement of days, months, and years in hours, minutes, and seconds.

The moon and the stars also play a very important role. From the moment of creation, they were set in the sky to light up the night sky.

Reflection

How many beautiful and significant things did God do for his creations?

The power and wisdom of God reveals to us that everything has been placed in its ideal place.

God's presence is the light of our days because it allows us to walk clearly without stumbling, as Psalm 27:1 details.

In the beginning, there was only darkness until God created the light.

In the darkness of sin, the light of God shines (Psalm 112:4).

Let's pray, thanking God for the time of learning His Word, and let's ask the Lord to light our path every day.

At the end of your prayer time, prepare the materials for the upcoming class.

IMPORTANT INFORMATION:

THEME: THE SUN LIGHTS UP THE DAY
BIBLE SCRIPTURE: Genesis 1:14-19

CLASS DEVELOPMENT:

Receive the boys and girls, taking their ages into account. Babies should be placed in cribs, playpens, on blankets or mats — depending on the classroom conditions. Then, welcome all the boys and girls, and indicate where the areas of play and other activities are (this is only for infants from 18 months). In this way, you can make sure that they'll be able to access the previously arranged material in an environment and at a suitable height for their age. This will also allow them to be able to share with their friends and teachers.

At the end of the play/activity time, gather all the children together, making a circle to pray and sing some songs to God, thus starting the lesson of the day.

Let's Talk. Go for a walk with the boys and girls around the church or the place you're meeting, and ask them to answer the following: "What is the day like? Is it sunny? Is it cloudy? We already know that the sun shines during the day; but sometimes there are clouds that don't let us see the sun. That's what it mean when the day is cloudy. When the sky is clear, then the sun shines on us in all its splendor and we can thank God for the sun."

Let's Play. Before class, make silhouettes of different shapes such as children, animals, the sun, the moon, stars, trees, flowers, etc. out of black paper. During the "Let's Play" time, hand out the silhouettes to the children. Then, ask the child who has the figure of the sun to hold it up, and ask the rest of the children to encourage the child by applauding for him or her. Continue requesting the children to hold up the different silhouettes.

Let's Learn. Remind the children that God created the sun to light up the day for us, to give us joy, and so we can go for a walk with mommy and daddy.

Activity. Provide each child with a worksheet and a CD. (You can use old, used CD's that no one wants anymore. Ask for donations from people in your church.) Instruct the children to color the picture of the sun. Then help them cut out their sun and paste it onto a CD. If you want, you can glue or tape orange or yellow acetate ribbon (ribbon used to wrap gifts) around the edges. (See example on worksheet.)

Conclusion. Pray and encourage the children to try to obey God every day.

THE SUN LIGHTS UP THE DAY

Instructions

Color the sun, cut it out and paste it on a CD. Then, glue or tape yellow or orange ribbon around the edge.

LESSON 21: THE MOON LIGHTS UP THE NIGHT

Biblical Basis:
Genesis 1:14-16

Objective:
To know that the moon was created by God to light up the night sky.

Class Preparation:
Teachers should meet beforehand to pray for the Class Preparation time. Then meditate on the verses listed under the Biblical Basis.

Introduction

Let's carefully consider the following:

Who made the lights and what were the lights made for?

What is the function of the lights?

What is the moon for?

Where did God place the moon?

On the fourth day, God considered that even light must have order and that what he had created in his sovereignty was good for his creation. Therefore, he very emphatically expressed the following: "Let there be lights ..." (Genesis 1:14), to separate the day from the night; and then these would serve as markers of sacred times, days, and years. Their specific function would be to light up the earth, to illuminate, guide, and direct in the midst of the thickest darkness.

The moon is considered a minor light, set by God in the expansion of the heavens to give light to the Earth.

Everything that God created is good for mankind and has a special purpose. Since its origin, the moon has been a great blessing (Deuteronomy 33:14).

Reflection

As we meditate on the Word of God, we learn that from the heart of the Lord, infinite love springs up for all of his creation. Even in our humility and limited way of thinking, we can see that God created many great and awesome wonders (Psalm 8:3; Job 5:9).

Let's pray, thanking God for the lessons he teaches us that we can then teach the boys and girls in our class and for the opportunity that we're given to also share these lessons with their parents.

At the end of your preparation time, prepare the materials for the upcoming class.

IMPORTANT INFORMATION:

THEME: THE MOON LIGHTS UP THE NIGHT
BIBLE SCRIPTURE: Genesis 1:14-16

CLASS DEVELOPMENT:

Receive the boys and girls, taking their ages into account. Babies should be placed in cribs, playpens, on blankets or mats — depending on the classroom conditions. Then, welcome all the boys and girls, and indicate where the areas of play and other activities are (this is only for infants from 18 months). In this way, you can make sure that they'll be able to access the previously arranged material in an environment and at a suitable height for their age. This will also allow them to be able to share with their friends and teachers.

At the end of the play/activity time, gather all the children together, making a circle to pray and sing some songs to God, thus starting the lesson of the day.

Let's Talk. Show the children the picture of the creation that you used in the previous classes, and point to the moon and stars, saying their names. Then ask the children the following: "Do the moon and stars shine on us during the day or night?" (Ask for volunteers to give their opinions, then continue.) "Have you seen the moon and the stars in the sky? Who made the moon and the stars?" (Wait for the children to respond, and continue.) "Remember that when the moon and stars come out at night, it's time for us to go to sleep."

Encourage the children to thank God for all he has created.

Let's Play. Before class begins, if possible, draw a large moon on the floor. If that isn't possible, make a large moon out of paper or material and place it on the floor when it's time for "Let's Play." Tell all the boys and girls to get inside the moon. Then, tell a story about the moon or sing a song about the moon.

Let's Learn. Remind the children that God created the moon to light up the night so we don't have to walk in complete darkness.

Activity. Help your little ones draw the shape of a crescent moon on a piece of cardboard or on a paper plate. (If you have a large class or think this will take up too much time, you could prepare the crescent moons ahead of time for each student.) Then allow them to color the moon. Cut out and give each of them the star that is on the worksheet and ask them to color it. Finally, glue a movable eye on the face of the moon, and attach the star with yarn or string. (See example.)

Conclusion. Ask all the children to pray together, saying, "Thank You, God, for loving us and caring for us."

THE MOON LIGHTS UP THE NIGHT

Step 1 – On a paper plate, draw and cut out the shape of a crescent moon.

Step 2 – Color the moon light blue and the star yellow.

Step 3 – Glue a movable eye on the moon and attach the star using a piece of yarn or string.

LESSON 22: GOD CREATED THE PRETTY FISH

Biblical Basis: Genesis 1:20-23

Objective: To know that God created the fish and everything that lives in the water.

Class Preparation: Teachers should meet beforehand to pray for the Class Preparation time. Then meditate on Genesis 1:20-23.

Introduction

Think about the following:

What did God command in these verses?

What species did God create in Genesis 1:20-21?

What was God's blessing on them (his new creations)?

On what day were these creatures created?

The seas were already created, and God saw that it was good. Then he commanded that they be filled with living creatures (Genesis 1:21).

God also blessed what he created and said, "Be fruitful and increase in number and fill the water in the seas …". This is a blessing that comes back around to bless people because through these wonders God provides for the needs of everyone (Leviticus 11:9).

In Psalm 8:8-9, we find that everything that exists in the sea magnifies the name of Jehovah our Lord because he is their Creator. During Jesus' time on earth as a man, fish were a major food source for many people.

Reflection

God shows us his power in the creation of the sea and all that live in the sea. Because of God's goodness, the sea provides us with food and is also a source of work for men and women. We must have faith and believe that everything God created is good, and we must take care of his creations and not contribute to the contamination of the environment.

Pray that you will be able to clearly share what you have learned with your students. Also pray for their parents, that they are grateful to the Lord.

At the end of your prayer time, prepare the materials for the upcoming class.

IMPORTANT INFORMATION:

THEME: GOD CREATED THE PRETTY FISH
BIBLE SCRIPTURE: Genesis 1:20-23

CLASS DEVELOPMENT:

Receive the boys and girls, taking their ages into account. Babies should be placed in cribs, playpens, on blankets or mats — depending on the classroom conditions. Then, welcome all the boys and girls, and indicate where the areas of play and other activities are (this is only for infants from 18 months). In this way, you can make sure that they'll be able to access the previously arranged material in an environment and at a suitable height for their age. This will also allow them to be able to share with their friends and teachers.

At the end of the play/activity time, gather all the children together, making a circle to pray and sing some songs to God, thus starting the lesson of the day.

Let's Talk. Prepare in advance pictures of fish that are cut out. They should be of different colors and sizes. When you begin the "Let's Talk" time, give each child a fish. Then, talk about the following: "Do you know what these pictures are? What are they? What are they for?" (Wait for the children's responses, and continue.) "Very good, they are fish! Who created them? Yes, God created them. All of the fish were created by God. Now, let's point out the largest fish; which one is the smallest fish? The thinnest, etc.? Where do fish live? They live in the water. How do fish move in water? What do we use fish for? They are food for people and they provide nutrition to help people grow healthy and strong." Then ask them to all move like fish and sing the song "God Made the Fishes"-3 Little Words-1st Volume (search on YouTube).

Let's Play. Have the boys and girls form a circle and sing the song "Peter, James and John in a sailboat" (3 Little Words or VeggieTales - search on YouTube). Next, invite them to play with foam rubber fish or fish silhouettes made from foam sheets.

Let's Learn. Remind the children that God created all the fish and that they are useful.

Activity. Provide each child with a worksheet and instruct them to color the fish. Then, give them cut out circles of assorted colors of cardboard or foam sheets and let them glue the circles on the fish like scales.

Conclusion. Pray, thanking God for another day of class. You can have the children pray along with you by repeating these words, "We love You, God, for the good food You give us every day."

GOD CREATED THE PRETTY FISH

Instructions
Color the fish. Then glue colored circles of cardboard or foam sheets on them to give them scales.

LESSON 23: THE LITTLE BIRDS SING TO GOD

Biblical Basis: Genesis 1:20-23

Objective: To know that God created the birds on the 5th day and they thank him with praise.

Class Preparation: Teachers should meet beforehand to pray for the Class Preparation time. Then carefully read the verses listed under the Biblical Basis.

Introduction

Let's think about the following:

According to Genesis 1:20, what did God command?

Where are birds to fly?

According to Genesis 1:26, who rules over the birds in the sky?

God created the birds, and according to divine order, they are to fly above the earth across the vault of the sky.

Man, God's favored creation, would be the administrator of all the creatures that God created and give an account to God for these wonders.

Birds, like all creatures, have specific characteristics that make them birds, but there are many varieties that distinguish them from each other and they live in many different places all over the world.

Most birds are defenseless animals that praise God through their various songs.

In Psalm 8, the name of God is magnified by everything He has created. Birds are part of creation and they require care, which comes from God (Matthew 6:26).

Reflection

Just like the birds, which are protected and cared for by our God, for the Lord provides for them so they lack nothing; so us humans, who are the favored creation of God, can live confidently in Christ. He alone is the one who provides us with all that we need according to his riches in glory.

To finish your preparation time, pray, giving thanks to God for the birds of the air and for the care that God gives to all of his creation.

After your prayer time, prepare the materials for the upcoming lesson.

IMPORTANT INFORMATION:

THEME: THE LITTLE BIRDS SING TO GOD
BIBLE SCRIPTURE: Genesis 1:20-23

CLASS DEVELOPMENT:

Receive the boys and girls, taking their ages into account. Babies should be placed in cribs, playpens, on blankets or mats — depending on the classroom conditions. Then, welcome all the boys and girls, and indicate where the areas of play and other activities are (this is only for infants from 18 months). In this way, you can make sure that they'll be able to access the previously arranged material in an environment and at a suitable height for their age. This will also allow them to be able to share with their friends and teachers.

At the end of the play/activity time, gather all the children together, making a circle to pray and sing some songs to God, thus starting the lesson of the day.

Let's Talk. Show pictures of different kinds of birds to the children, and talk about the following with them: "Do you know what these animals are called?" (Always wait for the responses of the little ones, and then continue.) "Yes, they're called birds. Who created them? Yes, God made them with his power. Very good! Now look at these (show pictures of different birds). What makes them different? What covers their bodies? What else do they have? They have beaks, feathers of different colors; they also have legs. With their wings, they can fly very high. There are big and small birds. And they sing to God; that is their way of thanking him for everything he does for them."

Let's Play. Instruct all of the boys and girls to get in a line. Then, have them raise their arms and try to imitate a bird flying. You can sing a song about birds flying in the sky.

Let's Learn. Remind the children that God created the birds and that he cares for them, especially the little wild birds.

Activity. Provide a worksheet for each child and instruct them to color the picture of the bird. Then provide them with feathers to glue onto the bird.

Conclusion. Pray, thanking God, because he will always give us what is good for us.

THE LITTLE BIRDS SING TO GOD

Instructions
Color the bird and then glue feathers on it.

LESSON 24: ANIMALS ARE VERY IMPORTANT

Biblical Basis:
Genesis 1:24-25

Objective:
To know and value the variety of animals the God created for our benefit.

Class Preparation:
Teachers should meet beforehand to pray for the Class Preparation time. Then carefully read and meditate on the verses listed under the Biblical Basis.

Introduction

Let's consider the following:

What did God command?

What species are detailed in these verses?

Why did God create the animals?

We want to take this opportunity to reiterate this precious event of the creation of the animals, and we can confirm once again that God has always existed and created the universe with the power of his Word. Let's also keep in mind that the Lord considers animals to be useful to mankind, and therefore, the Bible details the names and varieties of the animals.

Animals have lots of purposes. Some are companions or pets to people, such as dogs and cats. Others help with work, such as horses and cows. And some animals such as cows, pigs, sheep, chickens, etc. provide food for people. They all deserve care and protection because they are God's creation, and we have the task of being administrators and caretakers of them.

Reflection

How beautiful are the things that God created with the power of his Word! We must, therefore, teach these children to respect all forms of life, for the Lord created us all with infinite love.

Pray by thanking God for his creation and all we benefit from creation.

As you finish your time of prayer, prepare the materials for the upcoming class.

IMPORTANT INFORMATION:

THEME: ANIMALS ARE VERY IMPORTANT

BIBLE SCRIPTURE: Genesis 1:24-25

CLASS DEVELOPMENT:

Receive the boys and girls, taking their ages into account. Babies should be placed in cribs, playpens, on blankets or mats — depending on the classroom conditions. Then, welcome all the boys and girls, and indicate where the areas of play and other activities are (this is only for infants from 18 months). In this way, you can make sure that they'll be able to access the previously arranged material in an environment and at a suitable height for their age. This will also allow them to be able to share with their friends and teachers.

At the end of the play/activity time, gather all the children together, making a circle to pray and sing some songs to God, thus starting the lesson of the day.

Let's Talk. Try to find stuffed animals that make realistic animal noises, and show them to the kids. (We suggest that the stuffed animals be animals that are well known in your community.) Ask your little ones the name of each of these animals. (Wait for the responses of all the children, and continue.) Then talk about who created these animals and how we should treat them. Emphasize to the children that if they have pets, they must take care of them, feed them, and treat them kindly because they are also God's creations. Tell the children that we shouldn't play with them in a mean way or roughly and don't mistreat them, because they are not toys but living creatures.

End this time by encouraging the children to thank God for all the beautiful things he made.

Let's Play. Imitate the sounds that animals make with the boys and girls. You can also tell them to jump like bunnies and run like puppies. Sing the song "Old MacDonald" and encourage the children to make the animal sounds with you.

Let's Learn. Remind the children that God created all the animals and we must take good care of them. Some of them were even created to be people's friends, i.e. cats, dogs, horses, etc.

Activity. Provide a worksheet for each child. Help the children match the animal with the product they provide for us. Then, color the pictures.

Conclusion. End your class with prayer. Include prayer request that the children may share with you today.

ANIMALS ARE VERY IMPORTANT

Instructions
Match the picture of the animal with the product it provides us and color the pictures.

LESSON 25: BOYS AND GIRLS WERE CREATED BY GOD

Biblical Basis:
Genesis 1:28, 33:5

Objective:
That the children know that they are a gift from God and that He created them.

Class Preparation:
Teachers should meet beforehand to pray for the Class Preparation time. Then meditate on Genesis 1:28, 33:5.

Introduction

Think carefully about the following:

How does God view children?

What do children mean to God?

How do you think God felt when he "blessed them and said to them, 'Be fruitful and increase in number; fill the earth and subdue it.'"?

In Psalm 127:3, we find that "Children are a heritage from the Lord, offspring a reward from him."

Boys and girls are highly favored by our Creator. In fact, he gives them a very important place; for he considers them deserving of his Kingdom because of their innocence and sincerity. Jesus invited the boys and girls to come to him and he blessed them even though the disciples wanted to send them away. (Matthew 19:14)

Reflection

From the beginning, boys and girls have been highly esteemed by God, who is the Author of life and who considers them a gift for each family.

Hopefully, we have all enjoyed our childhood and were taught as children that God cares for each one of us. Blessed is the family that has children. However, there are homes where parents are unable to have children due to infertility. They should be encouraged by the church and taught that the Lord has given them the opportunity to parent spiritual children.

Pray that God will help us to value each and every child.

At the end of this preparation time, prepare the materials for your upcoming class.

IMPORTANT INFORMATION:

THEME: BOYS AND GIRLS WERE CREATED BY GOD
BIBLE SCRIPTURES: Genesis 1:28, 33:5

CLASS DEVELOPMENT:

Receive the boys and girls, taking their ages into account. Babies should be placed in cribs, playpens, on blankets or mats — depending on the classroom conditions. Then, welcome all the boys and girls, and indicate where the areas of play and other activities are (this is only for infants from 18 months). In this way, you can make sure that they'll be able to access the previously arranged material in an environment and at a suitable height for their age. This will also allow them to be able to share with their friends and teachers.

At the end of the play/activity time, gather all the children together, making a circle to pray and sing some songs to God, thus starting the lesson of the day.

Let's Talk. As the children arrive, put a name tag on each child (on their chest). Then go around the group of children and say each child's name. As you do so, ask the rest of the children to repeat each name followed by the phrase "is God's creation." For example, "Mary is God's creation." (Encourage all of the children to participate.) Next, ask the children to look at the body of each of their friends and say all together, "_____ has arms, legs, a head, a body, a face, eyes, a mouth, etc." Next, have them point to parts of your body as you say their name (nose, arm, etc). At the same time, ask them what each part of the body is for. (Wait for all the children to participate, and then continue.)

Emphasize to the children that God made us, and we must always thank Him.

Let's Play. Give each of the children a plastic or cardboard doll that has movable arms and leg. Instruct them that their goal is to make their dolls do the things you tell them to do, such as walk, jump, sit down, etc... Sing the song "Heads, Shoulders, Knees and Toes."

Let's Learn. Tell the children that God created all the boys and girls; therefore, we're happy and we want to thank God for each of them.

Activity. Provide a worksheet for each child. Then instruct them to color the faces. Provide them with modeling clay or wool (yarn) to decorate their hair.

Conclusion. Close with a prayer of thanksgiving to God for creating us, and pray for the specific needs of each boy and girl.

BOYS AND GIRLS WERE CREATED BY GOD

Instructions
Color the faces of the children. Then glue modeling clay or wool (yarn) on as their hair.

WEEK 13

LESSON 26: WHAT IS MY FAMILY LIKE?

Biblical Basis:
Genesis 2:21-24, 33:5

Objective:
To know that we're all part of a family.

Class Preparation:
Teachers should meet beforehand to pray for the Class Preparation time. Then carefully read and meditate on the verses listed under the Biblical Basis.

Introduction

Let's think carefully about the following:

Who created the family?

What was the family created for?

Who makes up the family?

Whose children are they?

Are children the property of their parents?

We see in the Holy Scriptures that God, in his infinite power, considers people the favored creation and therefore gives them great responsibility in taking care of and helping the world to grow, and their own family was part of this responsibility. So when God created the woman from Adam's side, Adam was very happy and said, "This is now bone of my bones and flesh of my flesh ..." (Genesis 2:23); that is to say that the man felt that he now had a helper and a counterpart to support a family that would include children.

Therefore, children are a blessing and gift that God gives to families. Children are not the property of their parents. Parents have been given the responsibility and the privilege to raise and take care of their children because they are a gift from God. (Genesis 48:9; Joshua 24:3)

Reflection

The family is the fundamental cell of society, according to the secular concept. This is true; for it is corroborated with the Word of God. In other words, the responsibility to raise his children lies with Adam. However, it also gives us the joy and responsibility of raising a family and being parents. The responsibility that God has given to parents is to raise their children in the love and fear of the Lord.

Pray for your time with the children in your class, for the children and for their parents.

At the end of your prayer time, prepare the materials for the upcoming class.

IMPORTANT INFORMATION:

THEME: WHAT IS MY FAMILY LIKE?
BIBLE SCRIPTURES: Genesis 2:21-24, 33:5

CLASS DEVELOPMENT:

Receive the boys and girls, taking their ages into account. Babies should be placed in cribs, playpens, on blankets or mats — depending on the classroom conditions. Then, welcome all the boys and girls, and indicate where the areas of play and other activities are (this is only for infants from 18 months). In this way, you can make sure that they'll be able to access the previously arranged material in an environment and at a suitable height for their age. This will also allow them to be able to share with their friends and teachers.

At the end of the play/activity time, gather all the children together, making a circle to pray and sing some songs to God, thus starting the lesson of the day.

Let's Talk. Have the boys and girls form a circle and ask them to sit on a blanket or carpet. Next, give each child a figure made of cardboard or form. Each figure should represent part of a family group, i.e. a mom, a dad, a child, a rooster, a hen, a chick, a bull, a cow, a calf, etc. Ask each child what figure they have. Then ask them to find their friends who have the other figures in their family group (i.e. the child with the mom will find the child with the dad and the kid.) Tell the children that God created families and we all have a family. We suggest you stop here and ask the children to think about and share with the class who their family is; i.e. who they live with in their homes. (Be sensitive to the different types of families that the children are a part of. Make sure no one laughs at anyone for not having all of the "traditional" parts of a family. Encourage everyone to participate.) Show the children pictures of different types of families, and sing the song "He's Got the Whole World in His Hands." End this section by thanking God for creating families.

Let's Play. Before class time, make up cards that have the different members of the family on them, i.e. daddy, mommy, brother, sister. When it's time for "Let's Play," distribute a card to each of the boys and girls and ask them to tell the class who is on their card. Then, ask all the children who have the picture of a daddy on their card to raise it high in the air. Then, have the children who have the picture of a mommy to raise them up. Finally, ask those who have pictures of children to raise their cards up. The object is to have all the children participate. Next, instruct the children to swap their cards with a friend, and continue playing until they can easily form families.

Let's Learn. Tell the children that God has created families with so much love.

Activity. Before your class meets, ask the parents of each of the children to bring you a photo of their family. Provide each child with a worksheet. Help the children stick their photo inside the frame (box) on their worksheet and let them decorate it. (They can draw their family, with your help if needed, if they don't have a photo.) You could provide stickers, glitter, or other fun things for them to use to decorate the frame.

Conclusion. Invite an older boy or girl (maybe a brother or sister) to come to your class and lead the class in prayer for the families of all the children who are present.

WHAT IS MY FAMILY LIKE?

MY FAMILY

Instructions
Paste a photo of your family, or draw one, in the frame and decorate the frame.

UNIT 3

KNOWING THE BODY THAT GOD CREATED FOR ME

WEEK 1:	I THANK YOU, GOD, FOR MY HANDS	84
WEEK 2:	I THANK YOU, GOD, FOR MY FEET	87
WEEK 3:	I THANK YOU, GOD, FOR MY EYES	90
WEEK 4:	I THANK YOU, GOD, FOR MY NOSE	93
WEEK 5:	I THANK YOU, GOD, FOR MY MOUTH	96
WEEK 6:	I THANK YOU, GOD, FOR MY EARS	99
WEEK 7:	WITH MY HANDS, I CAN TOUCH	102
WEEK 8:	WITH MY FEET, I CAN WALK	105
WEEK 9:	WITH MY EYES, I CAN SEE	108
WEEK 10:	WITH MY NOSE, I CAN SMELL	111
WEEK 11:	WITH MY MOUTH, I CAN TALK	114
WEEK 12:	WITH MY EARS, I CAN HEAR	117
WEEK 13:	GOD MADE ALL OF ME	120

LESSON 27: I THANK YOU, GOD, FOR MY HANDS

 Biblical Basis:
Genesis 1:26-27

 **Objective:**
To know that God made our hands and be thankful.

 Class Preparation:
Teachers should meet beforehand to pray for the Class Preparation time. Then carefully read and reflect on the verses listed under the Biblical Basis.

Introduction

Study Genesis 1:26-27 and then ask the following questions:

What does the Word of God tell us in the Bible Basis scriptures?

What is the origin of mankind?

We recognize that we're God's creation and that his love for each of us is infinite. We also recognize that we're saved by Christ and we're his church.

Read Colossians 1:15-23. Clearly, it is seen that there is a close relationship between God, Jesus Christ, and creation.

God created us to give him glory and honor (Isaiah 43:7). He knows every aspect of our lives; he knows us completely.

Reflection

Now, let's look at our hands (right and left), and reflect on these questions: What do we do with our hands? Do we use them to do good things? God has given us abilities to do good things, but we can also do bad things with our hands. Think about some things that you've done with your hands that don't please God.

Let's make a list of the good and bad things we've done.

We must make a faithful commitment to God to always use our hands to do good and avoid the things that offend God.

As you conclude, prepare the materials for the upcoming lesson.

IMPORTANT INFORMATION:

THEME: I THANK YOU, GOD, FOR MY HANDS
BIBLE SCRIPTURE: Genesis 1:26-27

CLASS DEVELOPMENT:

Receive the boys and girls, taking their ages into account. Babies should be placed in cribs, playpens, on blankets or mats — depending on the classroom conditions. Then, welcome all the boys and girls, and indicate where the areas of play and other activities are (this is only for infants from 18 months). In this way, you can make sure that they'll be able to access the previously arranged material in an environment and at a suitable height for their age. This will also allow them to be able to share with their friends and teachers.

At the end of the play/activity time, gather all the children together, making a circle to pray and sing some songs to God, thus starting the lesson of the day.

Let's Talk. Show the children pictures of people who use their hands to do their job, such as bricklayers, hairdressers, cooks, etc.

Then point out the following: "Boys and girls, I would like you to please show me your hands." (Try to get everyone to do it.) "What are they called? Hands." (Ask everyone to repeat it.) "All right, they are called hands! Let's all raise our hands and say this: These are the hands of _____." (Fill in the blank by naming a child in the class. Then continue around the room until you've said every child's name.)

"Now, what we can do with our hands?" (Encourage all the children to participate, then continue.) "We can write, clap, dress, eat, paint, draw, and much more." (Make motions for each activity as you say it.)

Let's Play. Tell the children to hide their little hands behind their backs. Then ask them "Where are your hands?" (Ask all the children to show their hands.) Then tell them that only the girls will hide their hands. Repeat the question and encourage the girls to show their hands. Do the same with the boys. Finally, do it one more time with everyone; encourage them all to participate.

Let's Learn. At this point, ask the children the following question: "Who made our hands?" (Encourage all the boys and girls to participate by answering, then continue.) "Yes, it was God who made our hands! Very good! Now, let's thank God for making our hands." (Lead the children in a prayer of thanksgiving to God for making our hands.) Then, tell the children that they'll be using their hands to do the activity.

Activity. Provide a worksheet for each child. Help the children put their index finger into the fingerpaint and let them decorate the hands by pressing their fingerprint onto the drawing of the hands.

Conclusion. Review the theme of today's lesson with the children, "Thank you, God, for my hands." Then lead the children in prayer, thanking God for your time together and being able to learn more about him.

I THANK YOU, GOD, FOR MY HANDS

Instructions
Put your index finger in finger paint and press your fingerprint on the hands to decorate them.

LESSON 28
I THANK YOU, GOD, FOR MY FEET

Biblical Basis:
Psalm 37:31

Class Preparation:
Teachers should meet beforehand to pray for the Class Preparation time. Then carefully read and reflect on the verses listed under the Biblical Basis.

Objective:
To know that God made our feet, and be thankful.

Introduction

Study Psalm 37:31 and 119:105 and carefully observe the following truths:

God directs our lives and illuminates our walk.

The path that has been set for us is safe and leads us to fulfill our purpose. So we use our feet to follow his will.

Now read Proverb 4:18, 26-27, and reflect on the following:

- We walk on a good path.
- With God's help, we won't stray.
- Bible reading and our devotions will always empower us on the path of good.
- Let's try to meet with the Lord every day.
- Choose a suitable place to pray.
- Request forgiveness for the offenses you've committed.
- Read the Word of God and meditate wisely on its content.

Reflection

Think about the following: What is your devotional time like? Devotional time is the primary way for a Christian to grow closer to God, and as teachers, we must make it a priority in our lives. In other words, we must ensure that our devotional time is a positive habit that contributes to our spiritual lives so that we can be a positive influence on the boys and girls in our class.

During prayer time, listen carefully to what God is saying to you.

Let's pray, asking the Lord to help us put into practice what we have learned; let's also pray for the lives of our students and their parents.

As you end this time of preparation, prepare the materials for the upcoming class.

IMPORTANT INFORMATION:

THEME: I THANK YOU, GOD, FOR MY FEET

BIBLE SCRIPTURE: Psalm 37:31

CLASS DEVELOPMENT:

Receive the boys and girls, taking their ages into account. Babies should be placed in cribs, playpens, on blankets or mats — depending on the classroom conditions. Then, welcome all the boys and girls, and indicate where the areas of play and other activities are (this is only for infants from 18 months). In this way, you can make sure that they'll be able to access the previously arranged material in an environment and at a suitable height for their age. This will also allow them to be able to share with their friends and teachers.

At the end of the play/activity time, gather all the children together, making a circle to pray and sing some songs to God, thus starting the lesson of the day.

Let's Talk. Show pictures of people who are using their feet, such as soccer players, cyclists, basketball players, etc. Then ask: "What part of the body are the people in these pictures using?"

Point out the following: "Boys and girls, let's show our feet." (Try to get everyone to do it.) "What are they called? Yes, that's right, feet." (Encourage everyone to repeat the answer.) "Now tell me, what can we do with our feet?" (Encourage everyone to participate in an orderly manner, and continue.) "Yes, we can run, walk, play, kick the ball, jump, take big steps or small steps, and much, much more."

Let's Play. Before the beginning of class, draw or somehow mark a straight line on the floor. As you begin the "Let's Play" time, start walking along the line and encourage the boys and girls to follow you. Then show them the route you took. Now, go along the line hopping from one foot to the other foot. Sing the song "Feet, Feet, Feet" (Kids Songs & Nursery Rhymes - The Children's Kingdom Nursery Rhymes; look for it on YouTube); and encourage the children to do the actions as they all sing together.

Let's Learn. Ask questions such as these: "Who made our feet? God! Yes, that's correct. God made our feet." Instruct the children to say together, "Thank you, God, for my feet."

Activity. Before class, use orange tissue paper to make paper balls by wadding up the paper. You'll need enough paper balls for each child to decorate their feet. During the "Activity" time, provide each child with a worksheet and instruct them to trace along the dotted lines to outline the two feet. Then let them glue the orange paper balls onto the feet to fill them in.

Conclusion. Pray thanking God for the time to be together and to learn from Him.

I THANK YOU, GOD, FOR MY FEET

Instructions
Trace along the dotted lines to make 2 feet. Then, fill them in with orange paper balls.

LESSON 29: I THANK YOU, GOD, FOR MY EYES

Biblical Basis:
Matthew 6:22-23

Objective:
To know that God made our eyes, so we can say "Thank you, God, for my eyes."

Class Preparation:
Teachers should meet beforehand to pray for the Class Preparation time. Then carefully read and reflect on Matthew 6:22-23.

Introduction

Read Matthew 6:22-23 and carefully observe the following truths:

What does this Bible Basis mean?

Why is the eye described as the lamp of the body?

The eyes are the organs that God has given us that allow us to see. With them, we're able to look at and enjoy all of creation.

If our eyes are healthy, we clearly see the objects around us.

If we cover one eye, how do we see? Well, we see differently and the true nature of things are not understood clearly. So…

Why do we need to see?

Is it easy to see in the dark?

If we have physical vision, we can see where we're going.

If we have spiritual vision, we'll have a life with direction and purpose.

Reflection

Let's think about this: how are our physical and spiritual eyes?

If our physical eyes are in good condition, we'll be able to live a good life.

If our spiritual eyes are working correctly, it's because the light of the Lord is in us.

Jesus said that when we have God's light in us, our eyes and our hearts are healthy.

Pray that God will help us have a good perception of the reality of the children in our class and of their families so that we can help them to be better every day.

As you conclude your time of reflection, prepare the materials for the class.

IMPORTANT INFORMATION:

THEME: I THANK YOU, GOD, FOR MY EYES
BIBLE SCRIPTURE: Matthew 6:22-23

CLASS DEVELOPMENT:

Receive the boys and girls, taking their ages into account. Babies should be placed in cribs, playpens, on blankets or mats — depending on the classroom conditions. Then, welcome all the boys and girls, and indicate where the areas of play and other activities are (this is only for infants from 18 months). In this way, you can make sure that they'll be able to access the previously arranged material in an environment and at a suitable height for their age. This will also allow them to be able to share with their friends and teachers.

At the end of the play/activity time, gather all the children together, making a circle to pray and sing some songs to God, thus starting the lesson of the day.

Let's Talk. Show children a large silhouette of a face with the eyes missing. Then say: "Boys and girls, look… I have two eyes." (Point to your own eyes.) "Show me your eyes and tell me how many eyes you have. Now, look at the things around you and tell me what this is that I am pointing to." (Point to an object in the room.) "What is this called?" (Give them time to think about their answers and the opportunity for everyone to give an answer.)

Let's Play. Instruct children to close their eyes. Then, ask them if they can see. Point out how difficult it would be to live without eyes! Ask them: "Without eyes, can you walk? Can you pick up things? It's really hard." Then let them open their eyes and show them pictures of people's faces and encourage each child to point to the eyes. Then sing the song "Two Little Eyes" by Godo Song (search on YouTube).

Let's Learn. Ask questions such as the following: "Who made our eyes? Yes, God made our eyes. Let's say together: 'Thank you, God, for my eyes.'"

Activity. Provide each child with a worksheet. Then, ask the boys and girls to color the face. Then, depending on their age, they can either glue movable eyes where the eyes go, or cut out the circles for the eyes and use it as a mask.

Conclusion. Pray, thanking God for the time to be together and to learn from Him. Thank God for our eyes and for all the beautiful things that we see with our eyes.

I THANK YOU, GOD, FOR MY EYES

Instructions
Color the face. Then glue movable eyes where the circles are or cut out the circles and use it as a mask.

LESSON 30
I THANK YOU, GOD, FOR MY NOSE

Biblical Basis: Genesis 2:7

Objective: To know that God made our nose and thank Him for it.

Class Preparation: Teachers should meet beforehand to pray for the Class Preparation time. Then they should carefully read and meditate on Genesis 2:7.

Introduction

Read Genesis 2:7 and observe the following truths:

How did God form people?

How did people become living beings?

People have two components: the physical and the spiritual.

The physical part is made up of chemical elements taken from the dust of the earth.

The spiritual part is what God breathed into mankind, "The Breath of life." God gives each person a spirit. That provides the life and the personality that makes the difference between a person and an animal, as well as other living beings such as plants, etc.

Mankind was taken from the earth and was made by the hand of God in his image and likeness.

Reflection

We're God's creation, and we have the power to be happy.

What can we do with our nose? We can smell perfumes, food, fresh air, etc.

What would it be like if we couldn't smell? Thank God because he has given us a sense of smell. We will always be grateful for his wonderful work.

Pray, asking God to help us see the good in each other and in other people. By seeing the good in others, we can encourage them to value themselves.

Pray for the parents of the children of your class, that they'll be sensitive to the goodness in their children.

As you conclude, prepare the materials for the lesson.

IMPORTANT INFORMATION:

THEME: I THANK YOU, GOD, FOR MY NOSE
BIBLE SCRIPTURE: Genesis 2:7

CLASS DEVELOPMENT:

Receive the boys and girls, taking their ages into account. Babies should be placed in cribs, playpens, on blankets or mats — depending on the classroom conditions. Then, welcome all the boys and girls, and indicate where the areas of play and other activities are (this is only for infants from 18 months). In this way, you can make sure that they'll be able to access the previously arranged material in an environment and at a suitable height for their age. This will also allow them to be able to share with their friends and teachers.

At the end of the play/activity time, gather all the children together, making a circle to pray and sing some songs to God, thus starting the lesson of the day..

Let's Talk. Bring to class items that have different smells (soft and strong) such as colognes, grass, flowers, garlic, lemons, etc...

Allow the children to smell the different odors. Then ask them: "What do you smell? What part of our body do we use to smell things?" Ask them to point to their nose. Then sing "Say to the Lord I love you" by agapelurve (search on YouTube).

Tell the children what the nose does, that is smells pleasant and unpleasant odors.

Now, show the children pictures of different animals and children, and in each picture, have them point to the noses.

Let's Play. Tell the children to close their eyes then put something (a familiar fruit, soap, etc...) in front of them and let them smell it. Then ask them what it is. (Encourage everyone to participate.) Ask them to inhale and exhale air. Place the children in front of a mirror and instruct them to look at their noses. Point out (using kind words) ways that each nose is different.

Let's Learn. Discuss the following: "Who made my nose? God! Yes, it is true that God made our noses." Encourage them to say together, "Thank you, God, for my nose!"

Activity. Bring to class pictures (or stickers) of things that have odor like perfumes, fruits, flowers, etc. Provide a worksheet for each student. Help each child trace along the edge of the nose and then let them glue the pictures around the nose.

Conclusion. Pray thanking God for the time to be together and to learn from Him.

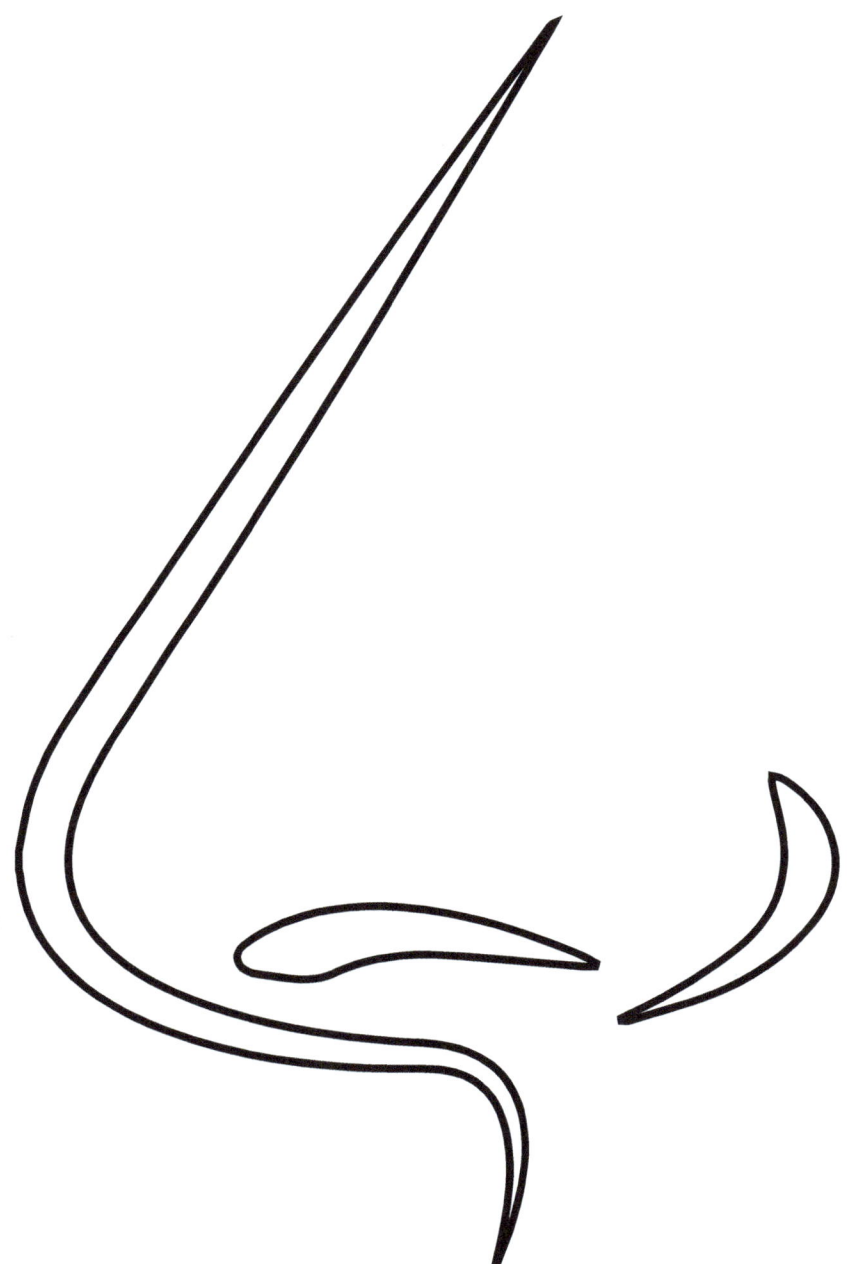

Instructions
Trace around the silhouette of the nose using an orange crayon. Then look for pictures of perfumes, fruits, or flowers; cut them out and glue them around the nose.

LESSON 31: I THANK YOU, GOD, FOR MY MOUTH

Biblical Basis: Psalm 8:2

Objective: To know that God made our mouths, and thank him for his beautiful work.

Class Preparation: Teachers should meet beforehand to pray for the Class Preparation time. Then they should carefully read and meditate on Psalm 8:2.

Introduction

Read Psalm 8:2 and carefully consider the following:

Some people believe that only noise or nonsense comes out of the mouths of children. This isn't so. Children have a fresh spirit and are ready to hear the voice of God and express what he is teaching them.

Let's remember that in the time of Jesus, children weren't appreciated, and it was considered a waste of time to spend time with them.

In contrast to the cultural norm, Jesus' attitude towards children was much different. In fact, he called the little ones to come to him and he placed them in a good spot: in his arms.

With the help of God and by obeying his teachings, we can use our mouths and tongues to reflect the presence of God in our lives.

Reflection

God has given us beautiful lips so that we can praise and glorify his name. Jesus calls us to serve him, and he treats everyone tenderly and lovingly. We must learn from the sensitivity of the boys and girls so that we don't miss what great things God may reveal to us.

Our life and our way of speaking must be pleasing to God.

We must be a good witness to our families, other teachers, and the children.

We must be willing to correct the children's mothers and fathers when they use negative words.

Let's pray, asking God to help us choose the right words when we speak of him and that through our mouths, our little children will feel his presence.

As you complete this time of reflection, prepare the materials for the upcoming class. Make a puppet whose face can show different moods. It should be able to look sad, happy, scared, etc.

IMPORTANT INFORMATION:

THEME: I THANK YOU, GOD, FOR MY MOUTH
BIBLE SCRIPTURE: Psalm 8:2

CLASS DEVELOPMENT:

Receive the boys and girls, taking their ages into account. Babies should be placed in cribs, playpens, on blankets or mats — depending on the classroom conditions. Then, welcome all the boys and girls, and indicate where the areas of play and other activities are (this is only for infants from 18 months). In this way, you can make sure that they'll be able to access the previously arranged material in an environment and at a suitable height for their age. This will also allow them to be able to share with their friends and teachers.

At the end of the play/activity time, gather all the children together, making a circle to pray and sing some songs to God, thus starting the lesson of the day.

Let's Talk. Bring the following to class: sugar, salt, coffee, and lemon.

Ask the children to close their eyes and tell them that you are going to give them something to taste. (We suggest that you give them small amounts, because some children are very sensitive to taste.) Then, give them one of the items you brought and observe their reaction. Ask them: "What did you try? How do you know? What part of the body helped you discover what it was?"

After each child has had the opportunity to try an item, ask them, "What can we do with our mouth?" Instruct all children to point to their mouths. Remind them of their answers, including that we use our mouths to eat, sing, speak, blow, scream, etc.

Now, show the children the pictures of animals and children that you used last week, (you may use as many or as few as you'd like) and ask each of the children to point to the mouth of the figure in each picture.

Let's Play. Enthusiastically ask the following: "Who can open their mouth wide? Who can scream very loudly? Very good!" Next, show the children a picture of a sad face and ask: "How do you think this child feels?" (They are sad.) "How do you know they are sad? Right, because of their mouth."

Let's Learn. During the "Let's Learn" time, ask questions such as these: "Who made our mouths? What do we use our mouths for?" Respond by saying: "You're right. God made our mouths. And we can eat, sing, talk, etc... with our mouths." Encourage the children to say together, "Thank you, God, for my mouth."

Activity. Before class, prepare enough speech bubbles for each child that are about the size of the mouth on the worksheets. On each speech bubble write "Thank you, God, for my mouth." Provide each child with a worksheet and a piece of red paper. Then, help the children tear the paper into little pieces and glue the pieces onto the picture of the mouth. Cut out the mouth. Then, glue one of your pre-made speech bubbles onto the back of each mouth.

Conclusion. Pray, thanking God for the time to be together and learn from him.

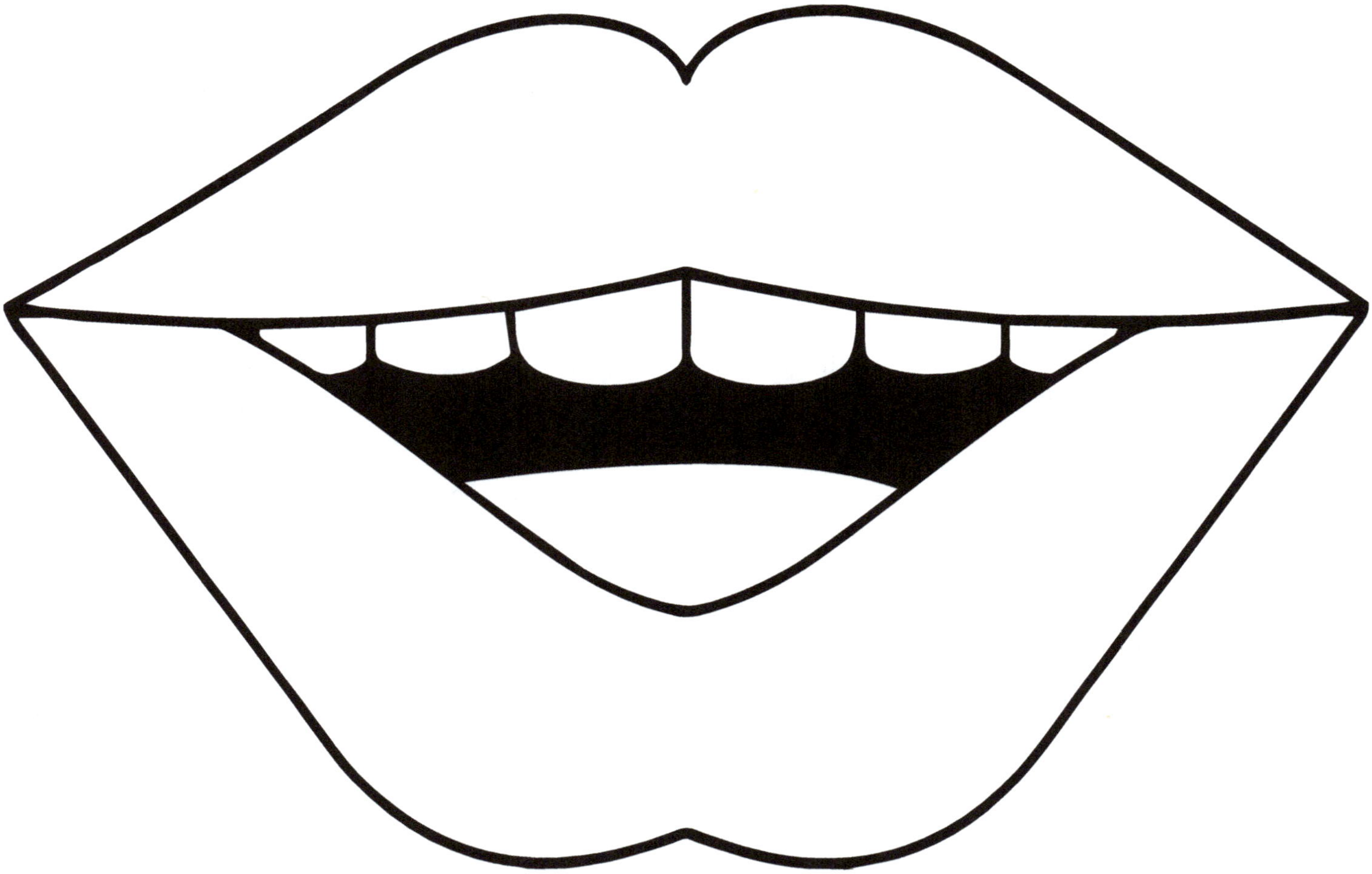

I THANK YOU, GOD, FOR MY MOUTH

Instructions
Tear red paper into little pieces and glue it onto the mouth.

LESSON 32: I THANK YOU, GOD, FOR MY EARS

Biblical Basis: 1 Samuel 3:1-21

Objective: To know that God made our ears and be thankful.

Class Preparation: Teachers should meet beforehand to pray for the Class Preparation time. Then they should carefully read and reflect on 1 Samuel 3:1-21.

Introduction

Think about the content of 1 Samuel 3:1-21 and note the following:

The ears are very important parts of the human body. They help us receive what others communicate to us so that we can relate to them. The inner ear is protected externally by the outer ear. Therefore, we must take care of the ears through personal hygiene. We can also take care of our ears by only allowing things that help our Christian life to enter our minds.

The Bible reading teaches us that it was not common during the time of Eli and Samuel for the voice of God to be heard. However, the Lord called to Samuel when he was sleeping in God's temple.

When God called to Samuel, Samuel replied, "Here I am."

God called to Samuel three times and then Eli realized that God was calling Samuel. Eli instructed Samuel to answer the Lord if he called a fourth time, which he did.

The Lord told Samuel that he would punish the disobedience of Eli's sons. The next day, Samuel didn't want to tell Eli, but Eli demanded the truth from Samuel, so he told him.

The Lord was always with Samuel because Samuel was obedient to God.

Reflection

Let's pursue a good personal relationship with God so that our faith doesn't grow cold. We must remember that God speaks to us at all times. Let's learn to listen to his voice and the message he wants to give us.

God is the same yesterday, today, and forever!

Pray, thanking God for this precious time and ask him to help us hear his voice and do his will. Pray also for the boys and girls in the class.

To finish your time of preparation, prepare the materials for the upcoming class. Make rattles from plastic bottles or cans. Place, in each container, seeds, pebbles, rice, kernels of corn, or anything that will make noise when you shake the container.

IMPORTANT INFORMATION:

THEME: I THANK YOU, GOD, FOR MY EARS
BIBLE SCRIPTURE: 1 Samuel 3:1-21

CLASS DEVELOPMENT:

Receive the boys and girls, taking their ages into account. Babies should be placed in cribs, playpens, on blankets or mats — depending on the classroom conditions. Then, welcome all the boys and girls, and indicate where the areas of play and other activities are (this is only for infants from 18 months). In this way, you can make sure that they'll be able to access the previously arranged material in an environment and at a suitable height for their age. This will also allow them to be able to share with their friends and teachers.

At the end of the play/activity time, gather all the children together, making a circle to pray and sing some songs to God, thus starting the lesson of the day..

Let's Talk. Bring different objects or instruments that produce sounds and hide them from the children. (The objects/instruments can include a cell phone, tambourine, music box, etc...) Once you gather the children together, have the different objects make their sound but don't let the children see the objects. Then ask the children what object made each sound. (Show the children the object and make the sound again as the children listen to it.) Repeat this with each object or instrument.

Ask the children what sound they liked the most. Allow time for each child to give their answer. Then ask them: "Where are your ears? Why do we need our ears?" (Encourage all the children to participate.) Then ask them to carefully point to their friends' ears. Ask them: "What kinds of sounds do we hear with our ears?" Review with them their answers and include things like we hear noisy cars, music, the voice of mom or dad, etc.

As you complete the "Let's Talk" portion of the lesson, show your class your pictures of animals and children that you used in previous lessons and ask the children to point to the ears in the pictures.

Let's Play. Teach the children the song "Do Your Ears Hang Low" (EFlashApps on YouTube is a good version) or use a song they already know. Explain that you're all going to sing with a very strong, loud voice. Sing the song again, but this time tell them that you're going to sing with a slightly softer voice. Sing the song a third time and this time in a very soft voice. After you sing, ask the children: "Were you able to hear what we sang clearly when we sang softly the last time? No, it was hard to understand, right? That's because we were so quiet. What happened the first time when we sang loudly? That's right, we could all understand the words. How do we hear? We hear with our ears."

Let's Learn. Ask your students: "Who made our ears? You're right, God made our ears. So, let's all say together: 'Thank you, God, for my ears.'"

Activity. Provide each child with a worksheet and some clay or play-doh that's skin colored. Instruct the children to glue the play-doh onto their picture of the ears.

Conclusion. Pray giving thanks to God for the time to be together to learn from Him.

I THANK YOU, GOD, FOR MY EARS

Instructions
Glue skin colored clay or play-doh to the ears above, or color them.

LESSON 33: WITH MY HANDS, I CAN TOUCH

Biblical Basis: Mark 1:40-44

Objective: To understand that Jesus healed a sick man with his hands.

Class Preparation: Teachers should meet beforehand to pray for the Class Preparation time. Then they should carefully read and meditate on Mark 1:40-41.

Introduction

Dig into the content of the Biblical Basis and carefully observe the following:

The leper begged Jesus on his knees to heal him.

Jesus said to him, "Be clean," touching him with his hand.

He had mercy on this sick man.

Jesus commanded the man to appear before the priest and offer sacrifices. This was necessary so that the man would be a testimony to the priest.

Reflection

How do we feel when we're sick? How should we treat others when they're sick? Who should we touch in the name of Jesus?

In the world, there are many sick people. Their illnesses, many times, are of a physical and/or spiritual nature.

What should we do for those in need?

How many parents of the girls and boys in our class are sick?

We must tell them about Christ and bear good witness with our own lives.

Pray to the Lord for people who are sick and for those who don't know Christ, that they may learn about him and receive salvation in Him. Also pray for the children in your class, that they will be a link between their parents and the church, that they might receive the spiritual touch of Jesus.

At the end of your prayer time, prepare the materials for the upcoming class.

IMPORTANT INFORMATION:

THEME: WITH MY HANDS, I CAN TOUCH
BIBLE SCRIPTURE: Mark 1:40-41

CLASS DEVELOPMENT:

Receive the boys and girls, taking their ages into account. Babies should be placed in cribs, playpens, on blankets or mats — depending on the classroom conditions. Then, welcome all the boys and girls, and indicate where the areas of play and other activities are (this is only for infants from 18 months). In this way, you can make sure that they'll be able to access the previously arranged material in an environment and at a suitable height for their age. This will also allow them to be able to share with their friends and teachers.

At the end of the play/activity time, gather all the children together, making a circle to pray and sing some songs to God, thus starting the lesson of the day.

Let's Talk. Bring to class a mystery box or black bag with different objects inside it. Be sure that the objects are things that the children will recognize by feeling them with their hand. Let the children take turns putting their hand inside, feeling for an object and telling you what it is. (We suggest that you always give instructions/rules of the activity clearly and specifically so that it is carried out in a pleasant, fair, and orderly manner.) (For ideas check out the website https://busytoddler.com/2017/06/mystery-box-easy-toddler-activity/)

Let's Tell the Bible Story: One day, Jesus met a sick man. The man was very sad because his whole body hurt, even his skin. No one wanted to go near him because he had a very bad disease. But one day the man approached Jesus, knelt before him, and said, "Can you make me better?" Then, Jesus said to him, "Yes, I can make you better." And at that very moment, the man was healthy. Yea! The doctors couldn't heal him, only Jesus could heal him because Jesus is so powerful and he loves everyone. That man wasn't sad anymore. Now, he was happy! (Look to see if the children feel happy and reflect joy on their faces, or if they feel sad. Pray silently, and let yourself be led by the Holy Spirit. Perhaps at this time God is indicating to you to intercede for the health of some of the children in your class or for the health of one of their relatives. Praying with children is a special blessing.)

Let's Play. Tell all the boys and girls to stand on one side of the classroom and put on their sad faces and say, "Poor man, nobody wanted to be around him!" Then, tell them to smile and hold hands with their friend next to them and say, "Jesus healed him and now he has friends!"

Now, have the children sit on the floor. Choose some children to come to the front so they can act out the Bible story as you narrate it. Be creative and involve as many children as you can.

Let's Learn. Ask the children: "Who in our story performed a miracle?" (Let them answer.) "Yes, Jesus healed the man. Because Jesus is God, he has power to make sick people better. Let's say together, 'Thank you, God for healing people!'"

Activity. Provide a worksheet for each child. Have the children circle the pictures of the objects that can be touched. Then ask them to color the pictures.

Conclusion. Pray, thanking God for the time to be together and to learn more about him.

WITH MY HANDS, I CAN TOUCH

Instructions
Circle the things that can be touched. Then color the pictures.

LESSON 34

WITH MY FEET, I CAN WALK

Biblical Basis:
Mark 2:1-12

Class Preparation:
Teachers should meet beforehand to pray for the Class Preparation time. Then they should carefully read and reflect on Mark 2:1-12.

Objective:
To understand that Jesus healed a man who couldn't walk.

Introduction

Think about the content of the Biblical Basis and consider the following:

Many people followed Jesus to hear the Word of God.

A paralyzed man was brought by his friends to see Jesus, but they couldn't get close to Jesus because of the crowd. So, the man's friends cut a hole in the roof of the house Jesus was at and let their paralyzed friend down through the opening they made in the ceiling.

Jesus saw the faith of these men and healed the paralyzed man. Then Jesus told the paralyzed man to get up, take his mat and go home, and he did. However, there were teachers of the law who murmured about what Jesus was doing.

Seeing this miracle, the crowd was amazed and they praised God. The people said, "We've never seen anything like this."

Reflection

Sin limits people so that they can't move forward because of the difficulties of life.

Jesus forgives us spiritually and heals us physically.

Jesus showed us his healing power when he was physically on earth, and he also shows it to us today, and he will always show it to us.

We can help those in need in the name of Jesus.

Pray, asking God for wisdom and guidance as you prepare for the upcoming class and for the boys and girls in your class and their homes.

As you conclude your prayer, prepare the materials for the lesson.

IMPORTANT INFORMATION:

THEME: WITH MY FEET, I CAN WALK
BIBLE SCRIPTURE: Mark 2:1-12

CLASS DEVELOPMENT:

Receive the boys and girls, taking their ages into account. Babies should be placed in cribs, playpens, on blankets or mats — depending on the classroom conditions. Then, welcome all the boys and girls, and indicate where the areas of play and other activities are (this is only for infants from 18 months). In this way, you can make sure that they'll be able to access the previously arranged material in an environment and at a suitable height for their age. This will also allow them to be able to share with their friends and teachers.

At the end of the play/activity time, gather all the children together, making a circle to pray and sing some songs to God, thus starting the lesson of the day.

Let's Talk. Start by singing "Happy All The Time (Inright, Outright, Upright, Downright)" (Find it on YouTube - Music Ministers Hub) and then tell the Bible story.

Let's Tell the Bible Story: Once there was a man who could not walk. He could not move his legs or feet. This man had four friends, and they wanted to see him walk. They heard about a man named Jesus and people said that he could heal sick people. So they decided to take their friend to see Jesus. But when they got to where Jesus was, there were so many people that they could not get to Jesus. So they went up on the roof and they made a big hole in the roof and then they lowered their friend down through the hole right in front of Jesus. When Jesus saw the man and all that his friends had done to get him there, He said to them, "I'm going to heal your friend." Then he said to the sick man, "Get up, take your mat and go home!"

Now talk with the children about the following: "Who healed the sick man? Yes, Jesus has the power to make sick people well. The man was so happy! Now, he could walk and run and jump."

Let's Play. Prepare an area with a goal and a ball for the little ones to play a mini game of soccer. It's suggested that you allow the children to play freely, but always — of course — under teacher supervision. After you've let them play for a designated amount of time, tell them to stop. Gather them together and tell them that now you want them to play without moving their legs or feet. Then have them sit down and reflect with them. Ask them: "Can you play soccer without moving your legs? Of course not. It is impossible to play soccer without moving your legs. Can you run without moving their legs? No, it's not possible."

Let's Learn. Ask the boys and girls the following: "Who did the miracle in our story? Yes, Jesus did the miracle, because he is God and God is all-powerful." Then encourage them to say together, "Thank you, God!"

Activity. Provide a worksheet, water color paints, and cotton swabs for each child. Instruct the children to paint the sneakers using a cotton swab.

Conclusion. Pray, thanking God for the time to be together and to learn more about him.

WITH MY FEET, I CAN WALK

Instructions
Paint the sneakers using a cotton swab and water color paints.

LESSON 35

WITH MY EYES, I CAN SEE

Biblical Basis:

Mark 10:46-52

Class Preparation:
Teachers should meet beforehand to pray for the Class Preparation time. Then carefully read and reflect on Mark 10:46-52.

Objective:
To understand that Jesus healed a blind man with his power.

Introduction

Read the Biblical Basis and carefully observe the following:

- The miracle happened in Jericho.
- The blind man was sitting by the road.
- He heard the crowd and was wondering what was happening.
- People told the blind man that Jesus was passing by.
- The blind man cried out to Jesus and the people rebuked him.
- The blind man shouted louder, "Jesus, Son of David, have mercy on me!"
- Jesus heard him, he ordered the man to be brought to him, and asked him, "What do you want me to do for you?"
- The blind man replied, "Rabbi, I want to see."
- Jesus healed him because of his faith and he immediately followed Jesus.

Reflection

The blind man had a desire to find Jesus.

When our desire is to find Jesus, we don't care about obstacles and criticism.

We must persevere in our cry to God and have faith that God hears us and will grant us what we ask of him.

We must be thankful and give God the glory forever.

Jesus is the same yesterday, today and forever, and he can do great things in the lives of each of the teachers and in the boys and girls.

Let's pray, thanking God for his Word and for everything he does in our lives.

As you conclude your prayer time, prepare the materials for the upcoming class.

IMPORTANT INFORMATION:

THEME: WITH MY EYES, I CAN SEE
BIBLE SCRIPTURE: Mark 10:46-52

CLASS DEVELOPMENT:

Receive the boys and girls, taking their ages into account. Babies should be placed in cribs, playpens, on blankets or mats — depending on the classroom conditions. Then, welcome all the boys and girls, and indicate where the areas of play and other activities are (this is only for infants from 18 months). In this way, you can make sure that they'll be able to access the previously arranged material in an environment and at a suitable height for their age. This will also allow them to be able to share with their friends and teachers.

At the end of the play/activity time, gather all the children together, making a circle to pray and sing some songs to God, thus starting the lesson of the day.

Let's Talk. Start this section by singing the song "Oh be Careful Little Ears" by Psalty's Songs for Little Praisers (search on YouTube).

Let's Tell the Bible Story: Once there was a man named Bartimaeus who couldn't see, and since he couldn't see, he couldn't work either. Because he was blind and couldn't work, every day he sat by the roadside saying, "Please help me, please give me some money." Sometimes people gave him a few coins. Then one day there was a large crowd passing by and Bartimaeus heard that Jesus was in the crowd. So, Bartimaeus yelled, "Jesus, please help me!" The people told him to be quiet, but Bartimaeus shouted even louder, and this time Jesus heard him, stopped, and told the people to bring Barimaeus to him. Then Jesus asked him, "What do you want me to do for you?" Bartimaeus replied, "I want to see." And instantly he could see.

Now talk about the story with the children. Ask them, "How was Jesus able to heal Bartimaeus?" Encourage the children as they answer and be sure to tell them that Jesus was able to heal Bartimaeus because he is God and God is all-powerful.

Let's Play. Tell the children, "Now we're going to act out the story of 'Blind Bartimaeus.'" Choose a child to play the part of Jesus and another to play the part of Bartimaeus. Place a strip of paper or cloth over the eyes of "Bartimaeus." Then have the rest of the children make a circle around "Bartimaeus." Have "Jesus" come into the circle and remove the cloth that is covering "Bartimaeus'" eyes. "Bartimaeus" can see! Encourage the children to rejoice and clap loudly because only Jesus can do miracles.

Let's Learn. Ask the boys and girls: "Who did this miracle? Yes, Jesus healed Bartimaeus so he could see. Jesus could do this because he is God and God is all-powerful." Encourage them to say together, "Thank you, God!"

Activity. Provide a worksheet for each child. Then give them some magazines and ask them to look for three pictures of three things that they have in their house. Help them cut out those pictures so they can glue them in the circles on their worksheet.

Conclusion. Pray, thanking God for the time to be together and to learn more about him.

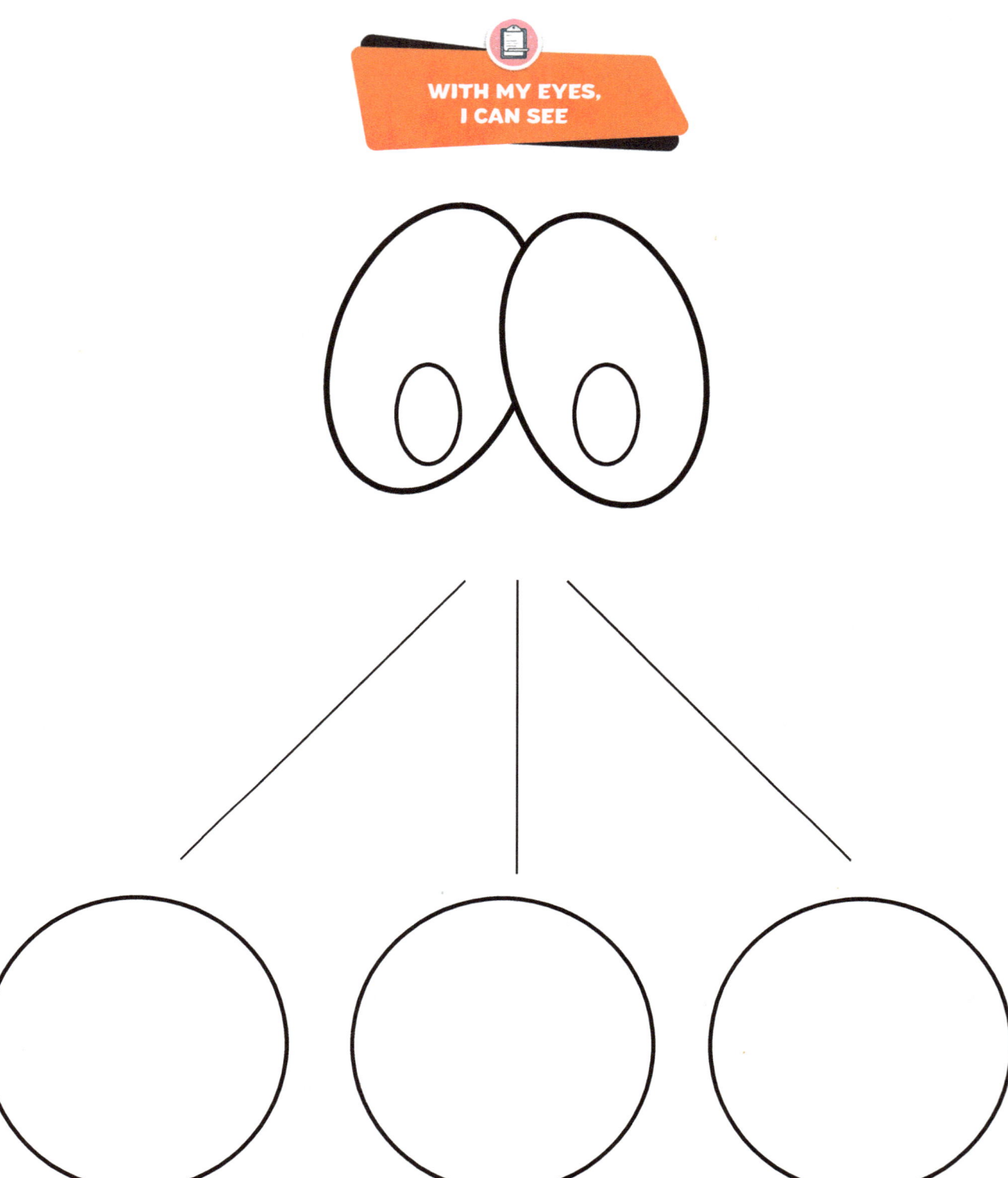

Instructions
Search in magazines for three pictures of things you have at home. Then glue them inside the circles.

LESSON 36: WITH MY NOSE, I CAN SMELL

Biblical Basis: 2 Corinthians 2:14-17

Objective: To know that we're a pleasing aroma to God.

Class Preparation: Teachers should meet beforehand to pray for the Class Preparation time. Then carefully read and reflect on 2 Corinthians 2:14-17.

Introduction

Think about the content of the Biblical Basis and consider the following:

What does this Biblical Basis teach us?

What does Paul compare followers of Christ to?

How is the word of God sometimes peddled?

What are followers of Christ to God?

Why was Paul thanking God?

What is our aroma to others?

How should we speak before God?

The life of the Apostle Paul teaches us many great things. We must try to teach these things to our girls and boys. In this scripture, it's necessary to consider Paul's character, sincerity, and well-placed faith in the gospel of Christ and his gratitude to God for all that happened to him.

Reflection

We must have courage like Paul did.

God is unchanging and helps us in all circumstances.

Our Christian life is like a pleasant aroma that reaches the presence of God.

Let's talk about Christ wherever we go.

Pray, asking God to use us as bearers of this great message to our girls and boys because they are a pleasant aroma to the Lord. Pray for the Christian education ministry in our church.

At the end of your prayer time, prepare the materials for the lesson.

IMPORTANT INFORMATION:

THEME: WITH MY NOSE, I CAN SMELL
BIBLE SCRIPTURE: 2 Corinthians 2:14-17

CLASS DEVELOPMENT:

Receive the boys and girls, taking their ages into account. Babies should be placed in cribs, playpens, on blankets or mats — depending on the classroom conditions. Then, welcome all the boys and girls, and indicate where the areas of play and other activities are (this is only for infants from 18 months). In this way, you can make sure that they'll be able to access the previously arranged material in an environment and at a suitable height for their age. This will also allow them to be able to share with their friends and teachers.

At the end of the play/activity time, gather all the children together, making a circle to pray and sing some songs to God, thus starting the lesson of the day.

Let's Talk. Let's Tell the Bible Story: Once upon a time, there was a man named Paul. Paul taught people about God and his wonderful power. He also explained to them that if we're good and do what is pleasing to God, we will smell good to him. We're like a very pleasant smell, especially when we share the Word of God with the people who live in our house.

So, we must talk about God and His love for us every day.

Let's Play. Bring things for the children to smell (i.e. apple, banana, gelatin, etc.). Make sure what you bring are things the children will be able to identify. Explain to the children that you are going to blindfold them one at a time. Then place one of the items in front of the blindfolded child and let them smell it. Then ask them to identify what they smell.

Let's Learn. Ask the boys and girls who made all these wonders, our eyes, our hands, our noses, etc... Tell them that it was our powerful God. Encourage them to say together, "Thank You, God!"

Activity. Provide each child with a worksheet. Instruct the children to draw a line from the picture of the nose to the pictures of the things that we can smell. Then color the pictures.

Conclusion. Sing the song "My God is So Big" (by Leylavis Christian — find it on YouTube) and end the class with a prayer.

WITH MY NOSE, I CAN SMELL

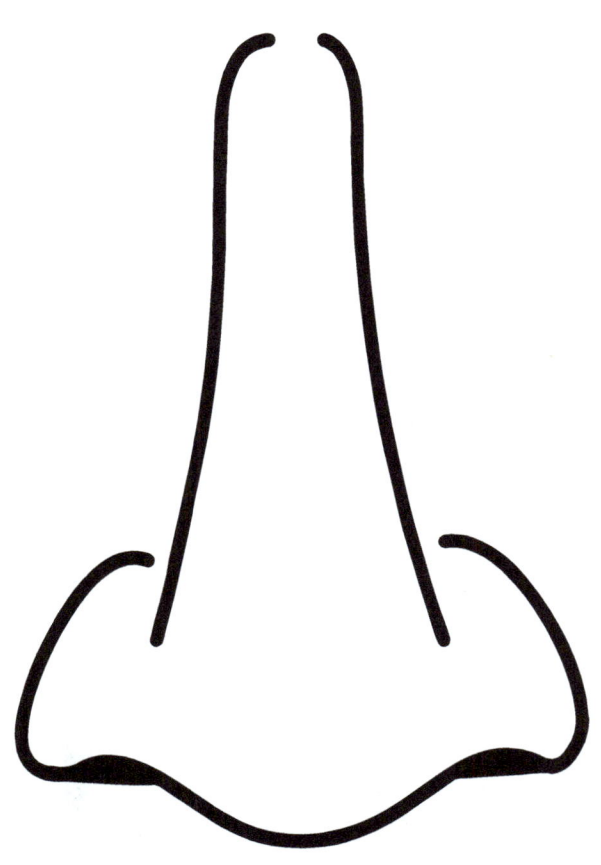

Instructions
Draw a line from the nose to the pictures of things that you can smell and then color.

LESSON 37: WITH MY MOUTH, I CAN TALK

Biblical Basis:
Mark 7:31-37

Objective:
To understand that Jesus healed a man who couldn't hear or speak because he is Almighty God.

Class Preparation:
Teachers should meet beforehand to pray for the Class Preparation time. Then they should carefully read and reflect on Mark 7:31-37.

Introduction

Think about the Biblical Basis and carefully consider the following:

The church makes itself known in its community so that it can help meet the needs of people with problems.

Sometimes, when Jesus healed people, their problems were solved.

A man who was deaf and mute was brought to Jesus. Jesus was asked to lay his hands on him and heal him.

Our Lord healed the man by putting his fingers into his ears and touching his tongue.

Jesus looked to heaven to give glory to his Father.

Jesus commanded them not to tell anyone about the man's healing. But the more he did so, the more they kept talking about it.

People marveled at what Jesus was doing.

Jesus has power forever. The world and everything created is subject to his will.

Reflection

Be thankful to God for everything he does in our lives. He can make us sensitive to the needs of those around us so that we can help them. As we help them with physical needs, we can share the gospel with them so that they can find spiritual help as well.

Pray, thanking God for the blessings we've received from him and for his love for all of mankind. Ask him to use our mouths to bring hope and the good news to those in need.

As you end your preparation time, prepare the materials for the upcoming class.

IMPORTANT INFORMATION:

THEME: WITH MY MOUTH, I CAN TALK
BIBLE SCRIPTURE: Mark 7:31-37

CLASS DEVELOPMENT:

Receive the boys and girls, taking their ages into account. Babies should be placed in cribs, playpens, on blankets or mats — depending on the classroom conditions. Then, welcome all the boys and girls, and indicate where the areas of play and other activities are (this is only for infants from 18 months). In this way, you can make sure that they'll be able to access the previously arranged material in an environment and at a suitable height for their age. This will also allow them to be able to share with their friends and teachers.

At the end of the play/activity time, gather all the children together, making a circle to pray and sing some songs to God, thus starting the lesson of the day.

Let's Talk. Start by asking the children why we need our mouths. (Encourage all the children to participate.) You should hear responses like, "To talk, to eat, to shout, to sing, etc." Reinforce their answers by repeating what they say if it's correct. (For instance, if they say "to smell," respond with "We use our nose to smell. What do we us our mouths for?")

Let's Tell the Bible Story: One day, there were many people around Jesus. Some people brought to Jesus a man who could not hear or talk. They said to Jesus, "Please help him!" Jesus took him by the hand and led him to the side. Then he put his fingers into the man's ears. Then he touched the man's tongue, looked to heaven, and said, "Be opened!" Instantly a miracle happened. The man's ears could hear and his tongue began to work and he began to speak.

Let's Play. Before class, prepare a paper bag for each child. Fill the bags with newspaper or something else you have handy that will make the bags round. Then on half of the bags, draw the top part of a face: the eyes and nose. The other half of the bags will be the bottom of the face: the mouth. As you begin the "Let's Play" time, give each child a bag. Once they each have a bag, tell them to find a friend who has the other half of their face (for example: if a child has the eyes and nose, he needs to find a friend with a mouth) and help them stick their faces together.

Let's Learn. Ask the boys and girls the following: "Who made it possible for the man who couldn't hear or speak to be able to hear? Yes, it was Jesus who is God, and God is all-powerful." Encourage them to say together, "Thank you, God!"

Activity. Provide each child with a worksheet. Instruct the children to fill in the missing part of the face (the mouth) in the pictures. Then color the pictures.

Conclusion. Pray, thanking God for your time together and for the opportunity to learn more about him.

WITH MY MOUTH, I CAN TALK

Instructions
Complete the faces by filling in the part of the face that is missing. Then color the pictures.

LESSON 38

WITH MY EARS, I CAN HEAR

 Biblical Basis:

Matthew 13:1-23

 **Class Preparation:**

Teachers should meet beforehand to pray for the Class Preparation time. Then carefully read and reflect on Matthew 13:1-23.

 **Objective:**

To thank God for the ability to hear and to be able to listen to Bible stories.

Introduction

Study the scripture verses listed in the Biblical Basis and think about the following:

What does this passage talk about?

In the "Parable of the Sower," what does the kingdom of God refer to?

Jesus was sitting by the lake.

A large crowd saw him and gathered around him.

Jesus got into a boat and taught in parables. One of them was the Parable of the Sower.

Jesus taught that the seeds were scattered in different places. Only part of the seeds fell onto good soil and produced a crop.

We use our ears to hear good or bad things. However, God helps us to listen to what is good and put it into practice.

Reflection

We're blessed to see and hear good things.

Some hear the Word of God and don't understand it, so the devil comes and takes it away. This is the seed that fell on the path.

Others hear the Word of God with joy but it has no root. So, when trouble or persecution comes they quickly fall away. This is the seed that fell on rocky ground.

Others hear the Word of God but are so worried about life and occupied with gaining riches that they are unfruitful. This is the seed that fell among the thorns.

Finally, the seed that fell on good soil produces crops that yield more than was sown. This seed represents those who hear the Word of God, understand it and live in it.

Let's look at our own lives. What kind of soil are we planted in? Do we produce a crop?

Let's pray, asking the Lord to help us have a spiritual life that produces good crops and that we'll help our little ones to be able to hear the Word of God and understand it, so they'll be fruitful in their lives.

As you finish up your preparation time, prepare the materials for the upcoming lesson.

IMPORTANT INFORMATION:

THEME: WITH MY EARS, I CAN HEAR
BIBLE SCRIPTURE: Matthew 13:1-23

CLASS DEVELOPMENT:

Receive the boys and girls, taking their ages into account. Babies should be placed in cribs, playpens, on blankets or mats — depending on the classroom conditions. Then, welcome all the boys and girls, and indicate where the areas of play and other activities are (this is only for infants from 18 months). In this way, you can make sure that they'll be able to access the previously arranged material in an environment and at a suitable height for their age. This will also allow them to be able to share with their friends and teachers.

At the end of the play/activity time, gather all the children together, making a circle to pray and sing some songs to God, thus starting the lesson of the day.

Let's Talk. Tell the children the following story, "Once upon a time, there was a brown puppy named Coffee. Rosa and Carl played with Coffee everyday. Coffee liked to play with his red ball. He also liked to eat his food and drink water. When Coffee didn't know someone, he barked at them to protect his home."

After telling them the story, ask them the following: "What was the puppy's name? What color was the puppy? Who played with Coffee? What did Coffee like to eat?"

Say to the children: "You can all answer the questions because you have all heard the story." Now is a good time to point out to them how important it is to listen carefully when someone is talking to them. When we listen carefully, we hear the full story.

Let's Play. Invite the children to participate in the activity called "Tell Me What It Is." The teacher will have five objects that produce sounds. Instruct the children to listen carefully to the sounds but don't let them see the objects. Then ask them: "What did you hear? What object made that sound?" (Examples of objects: sheet of paper, rattle, whistle, etc.)

Let's Learn. Share with the little ones that it's important to listen when our parents speak to us because this pleases God.

Activity. Provide a worksheet for each child. Instruct the boys and girls to put an X on the objects that produce pleasant sounds. Then tell them to color the pictures.

Conclusion. Encourage the children to say a short prayer, thanking God for their ears that allow them to hear.

WITH MY EARS, I CAN HEAR

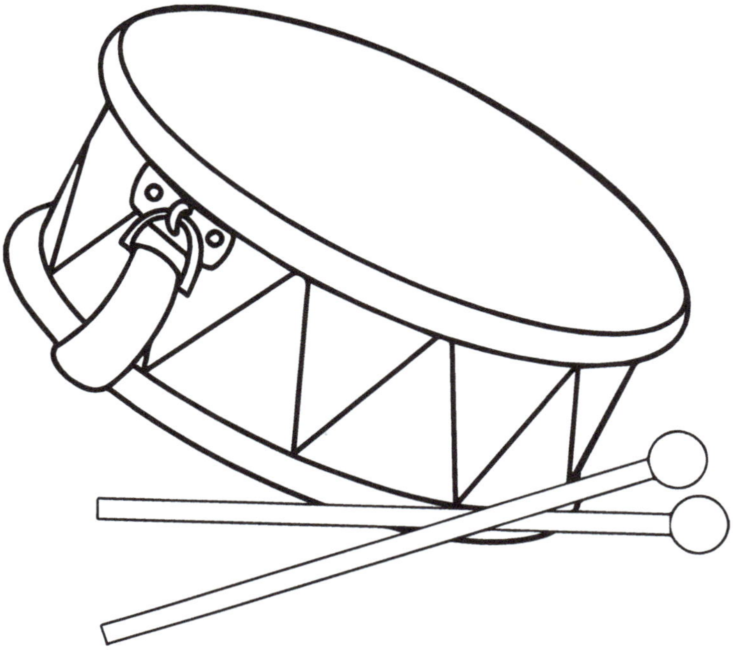

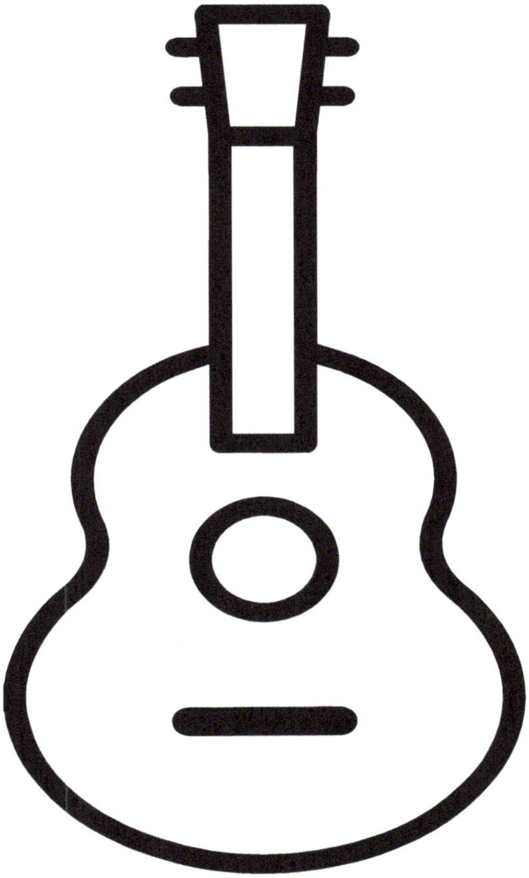

Instructions
Put an X on the pictures of things that make nice sounds. Then color the pictures.

LESSON 39: GOD MADE ALL OF ME

Biblical Basis:
Psalm 139:13-16

Class Preparation:
Teachers should meet beforehand to pray for the Class Preparation time. Then carefully read and meditate on Psalm 139:13-16.

Objective:
To know that God made our whole body, and thank Him for his wonderful work.

Introduction

Think about what the Biblical Basis says and then consider the following:

What does the psalmist tell us in this passage?

Who made each of us?

Where were we made?

How did God make us?

Before anything existed, there was God. His is from eternity to eternity. He is our creator and the author of life. He formed us in our mother's womb, he made us in the secret place. He has given us the privilege of being favored, and he has entrusted us with everything he has created. In the same way, our body and its functioning are subject to the will of God.

We're blessed by God, and he has given us so much. We must take care of the things he has given us, including our bodies, which are temples of the Spirit of God. The care of our bodies must be both internal and external to maintain comprehensive health.

Reflection

How gratifying it is to know that the body we have is the property of God and that its functioning depends on the will of the Creator. So, we must take care of it in order to have good physical and spiritual health!

Pray, giving the Lord your whole life to always serve him, and be grateful for all that he has done in you.

As you complete your prayer time, prepare the materials for the class.

IMPORTANT INFORMATION:

THEME: GOD MADE ALL OF ME
BIBLE SCRIPTURE: Psalm 139:13-16

CLASS DEVELOPMENT:

Receive the boys and girls, taking their ages into account. Babies should be placed in cribs, playpens, on blankets or mats — depending on the classroom conditions. Then, welcome all the boys and girls, and indicate where the areas of play and other activities are (this is only for infants from 18 months). In this way, you can make sure that they'll be able to access the previously arranged material in an environment and at a suitable height for their age. This will also allow them to be able to share with their friends and teachers.

At the end of the play/activity time, gather all the children together, making a circle to pray and sing some songs to God, thus starting the lesson of the day.

Let's Talk. Share the following with the boys and girls: "The Bible tells us about a man named David. He wrote about God and to God, and his words are recorded in the Bible. In one of David's writings, he said, "Thank you, God, because you made me; even when I was in my mother's womb, you knew everything about me. You made my body, my arms, my legs, my feet, my head, my face, etc. God, you are so good!"

Let's Play. All teachers should take turns being in front of the children, and they should make motions, encouraging the children to imitate them, while saying the importance of each of the body parts you present. For example, as you move your legs say, "The legs are used for walking, running, and jumping." The next teacher moves their arms and says, "The arms and hands are used to hug, clap, and write." The next teacher, "The mouth is used for singing, talking, shouting, and eating." And so on. Decide before class which body parts you will cover with this exercise.

Bring a large puzzle of the human body to class. We suggest that the puzzle be large and with only a few piece so that the children are able to complete it. Let the children complete the puzzle and encourage them to work together. When the puzzle is complete, ask, "Who made our bodies?"

Let's Learn. Explain that God made us. So we can say, "Thank you, God, because You made me."

Activity. Provide a worksheet for each child. Instruct the children to circle the picture that represents them (according to their gender). Then tell them to color the picture they circled.

Conclusion. Sing with your students the "Butterfly Song" - Heritage Kids (search YouTube). Then, pray thanking God for creating us in his image and likeness.

GOD MADE ALL OF ME

Instructions
Circle the picture that represents you (boys circle the boy, girls circle the girl). Then color the one you circled.

UNIT 4

JESUS IS MY FRIEND, HE TAKES CARE OF ME WHEREVER I GO

WEEK 1:	WE ARE IMPORTANT	124
WEEK 2:	EVERYDAY, I NEED JESUS	127
WEEK 3:	I'M LEARNING NEW THINGS	130
WEEK 4:	I'M LEARNING ABOUT MY COMMUNITY	133
WEEK 5:	I'M LEARNING TO USE MY BIBLE	136
WEEK 6:	I'M LEARNING TO PRAY	139
WEEK 7:	I SING TO MY GOD	142
WEEK 8:	THE GOOD NEWS OF KING JESUS	145
WEEK 9:	ANNOUNCING THE BIRTH OF JESUS	148
WEEK 10:	JESUS WAS BORN IN BETHLEHEM	151
WEEK 11:	THE SHEPHERDS WORSHIPED BABY JESUS	154
WEEK 12:	THE WISEMEN GAVE PRESENTS TO JESUS	157
WEEK 13:	JESUS, AS A CHILD, RECEIVES PRAISE	160

LESSON 40: WE ARE IMPORTANT

Biblical Basis:
Psalm 139:1-24

Objective:
To know that we're important to God, because He created us, knows us and fills us with His wonders.

Class Preparation:
Teachers should meet beforehand to pray for the Class Preparation time. Then carefully read and reflect on the verses listed under the Biblical Basis.

Introduction

After reading the Biblical Basis, think carefully about the following:

What does God know about each of his sons and daughters?

What does God understand and what does he examine in each one of us?

Where can we hide from God?

How and where did God form us?

What are God's thoughts like?

The psalmist David told us about the omnipotence (all-powerful) and omniscience (all-knowing) of God. God knows each of his children in the wisest and most perfect way that any being could ever achieve no matter how hard he tried. God is the Author of life and he created us, with love, to be important in this world. He frees us from danger and from those who want to hurt us. King David reminded us that no one can flee from his presence, so we must conduct ourselves appropriately, because the eyes of God are on all of us everywhere.

Reflection

God is all powerful in heaven and on earth.

God is everywhere. He was certainly present when we were formed in the womb of our mothers.

We could never run away from the presence of God.

The Lord gave us the blessing of being important, unique, and different.

Pray, thanking God for the children in your class and their parents, who are God's creation, and for the welfare of the families represented in you class. Then, sing the chorus "I Love You Lord."

At the end of your preparation time, prepare the materials for the upcoming lesson.

IMPORTANT INFORMATION:

THEME: WE ARE IMPORTANT
BIBLE SCRIPTURE: Psalm 139:1-24

CLASS DEVELOPMENT:

Receive the boys and girls, taking their ages into account. Babies should be placed in cribs, playpens, on blankets or mats — depending on the classroom conditions. Then, welcome all the boys and girls, and indicate where the areas of play and other activities are (this is only for infants from 18 months). In this way, you can make sure that they'll be able to access the previously arranged material in an environment and at a suitable height for their age. This will also allow them to be able to share with their friends and teachers.

At the end of the play/activity time, gather all the children together, making a circle to pray and sing some songs to God, thus starting the lesson of the day.

Let's Talk. Ask the boys and girls to sit in a circle on a rug or blanket (if that's possible in your classroom). The teacher should sit in the center of the circle. Then, gently place your hand on a child's head, and ask the other children to say the name of the child you have touched. If anyone doesn't know this little one's name, repeat it a second time. Then lead the children in a prayer, thanking God for creating them and that they will be healthy and can run and play. Continue around the circle, touching each child, saying their name and praying for them. NOTE: We recommend caution with this exercise if there is a child in your class who has a disability. If this is the case, we suggest that when you pray with each child, thanking God for his or her body, that your prayer would be very general.

Now take the children to where they can look in a mirror or bring a mirror with you to class. Tell the children that each of them will have the opportunity to see their face in a mirror. Then, let the first child look in the mirror and see their face, and at the same time, have the rest of the children say, "This is _____ and he (she) is special to God!" (Encourage everyone to participate.) Let each child have a turn looking into the mirror with the class responding. Then say, "We must remember that God made each of us special and he knows our names. Let's be sure to always be good children for God."

Let's Play. Bring to class a small, colorful, plastic ball that is easy for the children to handle. You will also need a way to play music and be able to start and stop it without the children being able to see. Ask the children to sit on the floor or in their respective chairs to play this game. This game is like the game "Hot Potato." Give a student the ball. Then, when you start the music, have the children pass the ball to the person to their right. When the music stops, the children must stop passing the ball and the child who holds the ball in his hands will say, "I am special to God!" Play for an alloted amount of time and then sing the song "Jesus Loves the Little Children" by atyourserviceable (search on YouTube).

Let's Learn. Remember that God has created us and we're special to him.

Activity. Provide each child with a worksheet. Tell your little ones to connect the dots to form bars to complete the baby's crib. Then let them decorate it freely.

Conclusion. Pray, thanking God for creating us and giving us healthy bodies that can move and play. (However, if you have a child(ren) with physical disabilities, we suggest that you pray, thanking God for giving us life and a body.)

WE ARE IMPORTANT

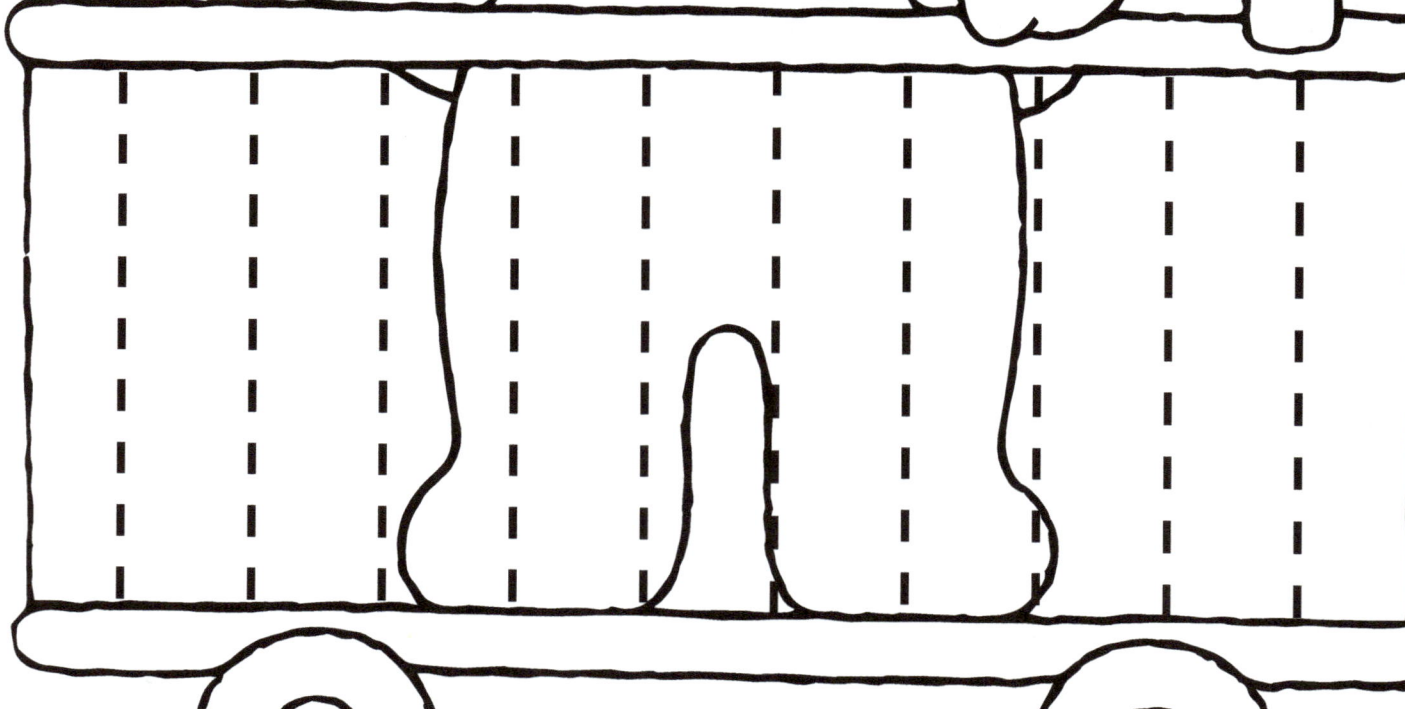

Instructions
Connect the dotted lines to form the bars of the crib. Then decorate the picture as you please.

LESSON 41: EVERYDAY, I NEED JESUS

Biblical Basis: Psalm 27:10; Proverbs 8:17

Objective: To know that we need the presence of God every day.

Class Preparation: Teachers should meet beforehand to pray for the Class Preparation time. Then carefully read and meditate on the verses listed under the Biblical Basis.

Introduction

Let's think carefully about the following:

How does God show us his care and protection?

Who does God love?

Who are those who find God?

It's important to know what the Word of God says about the value God places on his creations, especially how much he values boys and girls. They have special promises from God if they seek him, no matter their age. Obedient children who honor their parents will have long lives on earth (Deuteronomy 5:16). God never abandons them, even if they are abandoned by their earthly parents. It's very important that children obey God's commands (Proverbs 8:32). Children who keep and obey God's teachings are blessed.

Also in Acts 2:39, the writer tells us that the promise of forgiveness from our sins and the gift of the Holy Spirit is for whomever repents, for you and your children.

Reflection

- Our commitment is to help shape children to respect God.
- To motivate in children the desire to seek God from a young age.
- To prepare children to be obedient and ready to be part of the Lord's flock (Isaiah 40:11).
- To try to be a good testimony with your own life.

Pray, asking God to help us be a good testimony for the children and their parents. Let's also thank him that we're his blessed creations.

At the end of your prayer time, prepare the materials for the upcoming class.

IMPORTANT INFORMATION:

THEME: EVERYDAY, I NEED JESUS
BIBLE SCRIPTURES: Psalm 27:10; Proverbs 8:17

CLASS DEVELOPMENT:

Receive the boys and girls, taking their ages into account. Babies should be placed in cribs, playpens, on blankets or mats — depending on the classroom conditions. Then, welcome all the boys and girls, and indicate where the areas of play and other activities are (this is only for infants from 18 months). In this way, you can make sure that they'll be able to access the previously arranged material in an environment and at a suitable height for their age. This will also allow them to be able to share with their friends and teachers.

At the end of the play/activity time, gather all the children together, making a circle to pray and sing some songs to God, thus starting the lesson of the day.

Let's Talk. Before class time, organize/coordinate with teachers of other classes for a visit from your children to their class for this lesson. After all the children arrive to class, ask them to form an orderly line. Instruct the children to hold the hand of their classmates who are in front and behind them so that they can visit the classrooms in an orderly manner. Then as you arrive at each classroom, ask the children to greet each class and observe what they are doing. After you visit a classroom, ask your students: "Who were they? What were they doing? Why are they here? Were all of the children (adults) the same size?" (Encourage all of the children to participate; and then continue.) Explain that we all need Jesus, and in each class, teachers teach Bible truths that are very important for all of us to live as good and obedient children of God. We need God at home, on the street, at school, everywhere we go. So, we must pray every day as we get up and when we go to bed. As you finish up your "Let's Talk" time, sing the song "We Are Family" by Jack Hartmann or "Happy Happy Home" by the Superkids (search on YouTube).

Let's Play. Before class, prepare (buy, ask for donations, or make) puzzles that relate to children, family, or situations in daily life. Ask the little ones to sit in their chairs and put together the puzzles.

Let's Learn. Talk with the children about how we all need our God every day because he helps us live.

Activity. Provide each child with a worksheet. Help the little ones decorate the letters of the word JESUS and color the flowers.

Conclusion. Make two circles: one for boys and one for girls. Then assign a leader to each circle to pray for the needs of each child in your group.

EVERYDAY, I NEED JESUS

Instructions
Decorate the letters that make up the word JESUS and color the flowers.

LESSON 42: I'M LEARNING NEW THINGS

Biblical Basis:
1 Samuel 2:26; Luke 2:52

Objective:
To know that everyday we learn new things from God.

Class Preparation:
Teachers should meet beforehand to pray for the Class Preparation time. Then carefully read and meditate on the verses listed under the Biblical Basis.

Introduction

Think carefully about the following:

How did God bless Samuel?

What was Samuel's conduct or behavior like in his environment?

How did Jesus grow up?

What example does Jesus give us?

Typically when we talk about growth, we're referring to our physical bodies. But as we grow physically, we also grow or mature in our behaviors and attitudes, the basis of which we're taught from the first years of life.

Jesus, the Son of God, was a very special child. Every day he grew stronger, and he was also filled with wisdom. This allowed him to show the people around him that he was a child who knew many things related to God, his heavenly Father. And this wisdom surprised many.

Samuel was also an example of a good son. Samuel grew physically, but he also grew in favor with the Lord and with people, so God used Samuel as a prophet to his people.

Reflection

- Children are the result of what adults teach them. What they learn in the first years of life they'll never forget; therefore, it's important to teach them what's best for their lives.
- We must help them understand that everything comes from God, and to have the best life, we must always walk in his ways and trust him.
- We need to teach children that "The fear of the Lord is the beginning of wisdom." (Psalm 111:10; Proverbs 9:10)
- Teach children that no matter our age, our lives can be a good witness of Jesus.

Let's pray for the children in our class and for their parents so that together they may learn and discover new things from God every day.

At the end of your prayer time, prepare the materials for the lesson.

IMPORTANT INFORMATION:

THEME: I'M LEARNING NEW THINGS

BIBLE SCRIPTURES: 1 Samuel 2:26; Luke 2:52

CLASS DEVELOPMENT:

Receive the boys and girls, taking their ages into account. Babies should be placed in cribs, playpens, on blankets or mats — depending on the classroom conditions. Then, welcome all the boys and girls, and indicate where the areas of play and other activities are (this is only for infants from 18 months). In this way, you can make sure that they'll be able to access the previously arranged material in an environment and at a suitable height for their age. This will also allow them to be able to share with their friends and teachers.

At the end of the play/activity time, gather all the children together, making a circle to pray and sing some songs to God, thus starting the lesson of the day.

Let's Talk. Talk to all the boys and girls about the following: "What did you learn during the past week? What do you remember from our last class?" (Encourage everyone to participate; then continue.) "Every day, we learn new things. At home, mom and dad teach us; in the church our teachers and the pastor teach us. When we were born, we were very small and didn't know how to talk or walk; we couldn't eat without our mommy or daddy. But now we're learning to walk, run, dress ourselves, tie our shoes, go to the bathroom, etc. And every day, we do better. Thank you, God, for helping us grow and learn. He helps us grow and learn new things. As you grow, remember to keep learning and soon you'll learn to read, write, run, jump, cook, sweep, and so much more."

Let's Play. Before class time, draw or use tape to make two straight lines on the floor. Instruct the children to walk and then jump along the two straight lines. To do this, they must use their two feet and alternate them. After they walk and jump along the lines and have them walk on their tip toes and then on their heels.

Let's Learn. Tell the children, "Every day let's try to learn something new with the help of our God who has given us wisdom and understanding."

Activity. Provide each student with a copy of the worksheet. Bring old magazines or newspapers that the kids can use to cut out pictures. Help the children cut out and paste pictures of children doing different kinds of activities such as sleeping, eating, running, etc.

Conclusion. Tell the children, "Now we're going to pray, thanking God for the new things he has taught us in our class today.

Instructions
Glue pictures of boys and girls who are doing different kinds of activities in the space above.

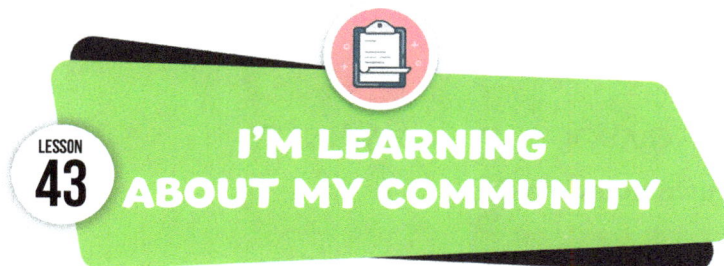

LESSON 43: I'M LEARNING ABOUT MY COMMUNITY

Biblical Basis:
Deuteronomy 6:6-7

Objective:
To know about, and every day value, the place and community where we live.

Class Preparation:
Teachers should meet beforehand to pray for the Class Preparation time. Then carefully read and reflect on the verses listed under the Biblical Basis.

Introduction

Let's think about the following:

As we grow up and get to know the world around us, we need the help of those who are older than we are. This may be our parents or other adults who take care of us and guide us on the path of good (Proverbs 22:6).

What does God teach us through his Word?

What kinds of things should we teach the little ones in our world?

Where should we teach and advise them?

When should we teach children?

All good teaching results in good learning. As they grow up, children learn about and become acquainted with the place and community where they live.

It's important to take advantage of their tender age to direct and guide their steps to the church of God.

Reflection

- Children learn from adults.
- We need to help children understand teachings that come from God.
- Children must recognize from an early age that God is their Creator.
- We should be telling others what God has done in our life.

Let's pray for the children, their parents, and for help to teach them with power and love what God wants for them.

At the end of your preparation time, prepare the materials for the upcoming lesson.

IMPORTANT INFORMATION:

THEME: I'M LEARNING ABOUT MY COMMUNITY
BIBLE SCRIPTURE: Deuteronomy 6:6-7

CLASS DEVELOPMENT:

Receive the boys and girls, taking their ages into account. Babies should be placed in cribs, playpens, on blankets or mats — depending on the classroom conditions. Then, welcome all the boys and girls, and indicate where the areas of play and other activities are (this is only for infants from 18 months). In this way, you can make sure that they'll be able to access the previously arranged material in an environment and at a suitable height for their age. This will also allow them to be able to share with their friends and teachers.

At the end of the play/activity time, gather all the children together, making a circle to pray and sing some songs to God, thus starting the lesson of the day.

Let's Talk. Show your class a picture of a city or community where houses are clearly visible. Then talk about the picture by asking: "What do you see in the picture? What are they called? That's right, houses. What are they like? Do they have doors? What else do they have? Do they have gardens? Do you like all of them? Do they look like your house?" (Try to get everyone involved, and then continue.) "Do you know who lives in these houses? No, we don't know, but God knows. He knows everything because he is God. He also knows where you and all the boys and girls in our class live. And do you know where you live? Do you know the name of the street you live on? Let's all go home and ask our mommy and daddy the name of our street, and in the next class, we will all share the name of the street that we live on."

Let's Play. Before class, ask for parental permission to take the children for a walk down the street the church is on. (You may need to have permissions slips with the parents signature on it.) Also, organize some extra teachers who can come along with you for extra help and safety of the children.

Organize the children so you can go for a walk. Walk along the streets near the church. Point out different houses and their unique attributes. (I.e. That house has a brown door or that house has lots of beautiful flowers, etc.)

Let's Learn. Tell the children: "Every day let's try to learn something new with the help of our God who has given us wisdom and understanding."

Activity. Provide each child with a worksheet. Instruct them to draw a circle around the pictures that represent places in their community that they like to go to, and color them.

Conclusion. Pray for each of the requests that the boys and girls have shared.

Instructions
Draw a circle around the places in your community that you like to visit. Then color them.

LESSON 44

I'M LEARNING TO USE MY BIBLE

Biblical Basis:
Psalms 119:105

Objective:
To know that the Bible is the Word of God that guides and teaches us.

Class Preparation:
Teachers should meet beforehand to pray for the Class Preparation time. Then carefully read and meditate on the verses listed under the Biblical Basis.

Introduction

Let's think carefully about the following:

What does the psalmist tell us about the Word of God?

What does the Word of God represent in our lives?

Why does the Word of God enlighten us?

The psalmist wrote from the depths of his heart to tell us that the holy Word of God transforms our life; it helps us make ourselves better by, "… making wise the simple" (Psalm 19:7).

We must encourage children to learn to read and get to know their Bibles from the first years of their lives. We must use and treat the Bible with great respect because it is God's Word, which teaches us how to live a life worthy of his love.

The apostle Paul encouraged Timothy to persist in what he learned in Holy Scripture as a child (2 Timothy 3:15).

Reflection

- God left us His Word so that through it we may be equipped to lead others to him. (2 Timothy 3:16)
- It's important that we get to know what the Holy Bible says and means and that we abide by what it teaches us.
- Teachers should be good models of how we're to read and use the Bible.
- We must try to teach God's Word appropriately to the children in the class.

Pray for the children in your class and their parents, that they'll understand that God's love is true and faithful.

As you conclude your prayer time, prepare the materials for the upcoming class.

IMPORTANT INFORMATION:

THEME: I'M LEARNING TO USE MY BIBLE

BIBLE SCRIPTURE: Psalms 119:105

CLASS DEVELOPMENT:

Receive the boys and girls, taking their ages into account. Babies should be placed in cribs, playpens, on blankets or mats — depending on the classroom conditions. Then, welcome all the boys and girls, and indicate where the areas of play and other activities are (this is only for infants from 18 months). In this way, you can make sure that they'll be able to access the previously arranged material in an environment and at a suitable height for their age. This will also allow them to be able to share with their friends and teachers.

At the end of the play/activity time, gather all the children together, making a circle to pray and sing some songs to God, thus starting the lesson of the day.

Let's Talk. Place several copies of the Bible or New Testament on the tables or in the cabinets around your classroom. Make these Bibles available for the children to hold and look through. Since your children are toddlers, picture Bibles would be ideal. As you begin class, point out the Bibles and their location to the children, then take a Bible in your hands and talk with them about the following: "What is this book called? Do you know what it is? Have you ever seen a Bible before?" Now, instruct each child to hold a Bible in their hands, and say: "This book is called the Bible. It is the Word of God. It tells us about people who lived a long time ago. They were very good and love God a lot. They teach us to live like God wants us to. The Bible is a very special book. God speaks to us through His book."

Let's Play. Instruct the children to make a circle and teach them the song "The B-I-B-L-E" (search on YouTube). Then have them walk along a line or around a rug placed on the floor carrying a Bible under their arm. Have them repeat after you, "This book is special, it's the Word of God."

Let's Learn. Remind the children that God speaks to us through His Word, the Holy Bible.

Activity. Provide a worksheet for each child. Give them time to color the picture while they listen to the song "The B-I-B-L-E."

Conclusion. End this class time by thanking God for giving us His Word that teaches us about His love for us.

I'M LEARNING TO USE MY BIBLE

Instructions
Color the picture.

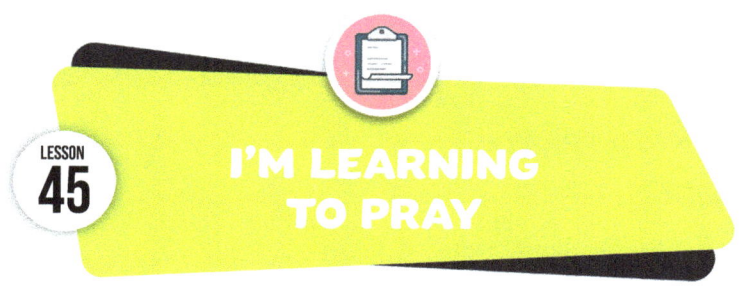

LESSON 45 — I'M LEARNING TO PRAY

Biblical Basis:
Psalm 65:2

Class Preparation:
Teachers should meet beforehand to pray for the Class Preparation time. Then carefully read and meditate on the verses listed under the Biblical Basis.

Objective:
To know that prayer is a real and direct conversation with God.

Introduction

Let's think carefully about the following:

Why did David express himself this way?

Is it necessary to pray?

Who should pray?

The psalmist recognized that if we pray faithfully, God hears our prayers and takes them to heart. Therefore, it's important that we pray and that we teach others how to pray. Jesus taught his disciples, and us, to pray when he taught the disciples the "Lord's Prayer." The Bible tells us that Jesus frequently prayed to his Father at various times and in various places. Prayer is a necessity in the life of a Christian. The Holy Spirit helps us in our weakness by interceding for us (Romans 8:26).

Through prayer, we can ask God for forgiveness and he will forgive us.

Reflection

If we ask God for something in prayer, we have the complete assurance that He listens to us. Prayer also brings blessings to our lives.

We must help the children in our class form good habits of praying in all situations, having faith that God hears our prayers, and knowing that he is attentive to what we ask and need.

Pray for the children in your class and for their parents. Pray that the parents will pray every day, demonstrating good prayer habits to their children.

At the end of your prayer time, prepare the materials for the following lesson.

IMPORTANT INFORMATION:

THEME: I'M LEARNING TO PRAY
BIBLE SCRIPTURE: Psalm 65:2

CLASS DEVELOPMENT:

Receive the boys and girls, taking their ages into account. Babies should be placed in cribs, playpens, on blankets or mats — depending on the classroom conditions. Then, welcome all the boys and girls, and indicate where the areas of play and other activities are (this is only for infants from 18 months). In this way, you can make sure that they'll be able to access the previously arranged material in an environment and at a suitable height for their age. This will also allow them to be able to share with their friends and teachers.

At the end of the play/activity time, gather all the children together, making a circle to pray and sing some songs to God, thus starting the lesson of the day.

Let's Talk. Ask the children, one at a time, to tell the class their name. (Encourage everyone to participate.) Then say something like: "Thank you so much for sharing your names with us. Isn't it wonderful that we all know how to speak, and you all do it very well. Have you noticed that I (if there are multiple teachers say "we" and point to the teachers) can also speak. And when I (we) speak, you all listen and answer if a question is asked." Show the children a copy of the New Testament and say: "You already know about this book. What is it called? It's name is…, (the Bible) and in it we're told about God's love and how we can talk with Him. How do we talk to God? (Through prayer) And when should we talk to God? (Every day) Do we pray alone? (Sometimes alone and sometimes with mommy and daddy or others.) What parts of the day are good times to pray? (In the morning, when we eat, and at bedtime.)"

Let's Play. If possible, show the children the video and teach them the song "I Will Pray" by Justis Zietlow (search YouTube). Then lead your class in prayer. Direct the children to repeat what you say and to pray from the bottom of their hearts.

Let's Learn. Tell the children that God speaks to us through prayer.

Activity. Provide a worksheet for each child. Allow the children to color the picture however they'd like and then have them say together, "I'm learning to pray."

Conclusion. As you conclude the class, have the children stand in a circle and thank God for listening to and answering our prayers.

I'M LEARNING TO PRAY

Instructions
Color the picture and then say the following: "I'm learning to pray."

LESSON 46: I SING TO MY GOD

Biblical Basis:
Psalm 96:1-3

Objective:
To know that it's important to sing to God, thanking Him for the wonderful things He does in our lives.

Class Preparation:
Teachers should meet beforehand to pray for the Class Preparation time. Then carefully read and reflect on the verses listed under the Biblical Basis.

Introduction

Let's think about the following:

How should God be sung to?

Who should sing to him?

What should we say when we sing to God?

Who will worship and sing to him?

According to the Bible, singing is a wonderful way that we can praise God. When we sing to God, we should sing joyfully (Psalm 81:1). Our songs to God should be sung with joy because he is the rock of our salvation, the Mighty One of Israel.

God's children are called to sing to him and to do so with a willing and understanding heart.

Praise is a way we can worship the Creator, and we can also do it with musical instruments. In fact, the Bible talks about instruments that were used in Bible times to worship the Lord. The Bible urges us to praise God with all we are and have.

Reflection

- As we teach our students about praise, let our praise come from the bottom of our hearts.
- May we instill in children that praise is a way of worshiping the almighty God who is worthy of all praise.
- We, as teachers, need to be true models of how to worship God.

Pray for the children in your class and for their parents. Thank God for the precious time he gives us to be able to teach these little ones the importance of having a habit of praise.

At the end of your prayer time, prepare the materials for the following class.

IMPORTANT INFORMATION:

THEME: I SING TO MY GOD
BIBLE SCRIPTURE: Psalm 96:1-3

CLASS DEVELOPMENT:

Receive the boys and girls, taking their ages into account. Babies should be placed in cribs, playpens, on blankets or mats — depending on the classroom conditions. Then, welcome all the boys and girls, and indicate where the areas of play and other activities are (this is only for infants from 18 months). In this way, you can make sure that they'll be able to access the previously arranged material in an environment and at a suitable height for their age. This will also allow them to be able to share with their friends and teachers.

At the end of the play/activity time, gather all the children together, making a circle to pray and sing some songs to God, thus starting the lesson of the day.

Let's Talk. Talk with the boys and girls about the following: "How are you today? What have you been doing?" (Encourage everyone to express themselves, and then continue.) "Are you happy today? I'm happy. Do you know why I'm happy? It's because we're all children of God. He loves us so much! And isn't it wonderful that he has given us a mouth?" (Ask the children to point to their mouth.) "With our mouth we can talk, laugh, and sing. God wants us to be happy in his house, the church, and because we're happy, we can praise him by thanking him." Lead the children in the chorus "Give Thanks to the Lord" (search YouTube). After you sing the song say: "Isn't it good to know that we can sing songs to God and thank him for all the nice things he has done, especially for creating all of us. We're important to God, so let's remember to sing praises to him."

Let's Play. Leave the classroom in an orderly manner with the children, asking them to hold hands. Make sure that you are someplace where you won't disturb other classes. Have the children form a circle and then sing the following song with them, accompanied by actions: "Praise the Lord Every Day" by PBC Creation Station (search on YouTube).

Let's Learn. Return to the classroom and share with your little ones that it's wonderful to praise God; through praise, we worship him for all the beauty he has created.

Activity. Before class time, ask parents to send an old, large shirt that can be used as a paint shirt to cover their child's nice clothes so they can paint. Help each child put on his or her paint shirt and then provide the child with a worksheet and let them paint it however they'd like. (It would be a good idea to have a few extra paint shirts for those whose parents might forget or for visitors.)

Conclusion. Conclude the class by asking the children if they have anything they would like you to pray about, and include those requests in the closing prayer. Thank God because we can praise him, and for the time of being able to share together and learn more about him.

I SING TO MY GOD

Instructions
Paint the picture and use lots of different colors.

LESSON 47

THE GOOD NEWS OF KING JESUS

Biblical Basis:
Isaiah 52:7; John 1:6-14

Objective:
To know that the Bible announced the arrival of the Savior.

Class Preparation:
Teachers should meet beforehand to pray for the Class Preparation time. Then carefully read and meditate on the verses listed under the Biblical Basis.

Introduction

Think carefully about the following:

What did the writer of the book of Isaiah mean?

How are the feet of the one who brings good news described?

Who sent John the Baptist?

What or who was John testifying about?

Who was "that light"?

Good news is always a cause of joy and happiness to the person or the group of people who deliver it, as well as to those who receive it.

The Bible tells us about a prophecy that was announced many years before it came to pass, and it was received with delight and wonder. People who were charged with sharing the Good News of the Savior's arrival did so with excitement. Even though they didn't know when it would happen, the news was full of promise. Many years later, Jesus — the King of the Jews — came, but his coming wasn't what the people expected.

John the Baptist testified to the light that was Christ the Savior.

Reflection

- It's important to know that God ordained all things to bless his children! We must always be thankful to the Lord, for he loves us and cares about us.
- The arrival of the Savior was the Greatest News in history. We must never forget this event that means we can have redemption in our lives.
- The most important thing we can do is announce to the world that Jesus is the true light and he will give light to those who live in darkness. Let's follow that light!

Let's pray for this precious time with these children and for their parents; that everyone will come to understand the truth.

At the end of your preparation time, prepare the materials for the upcoming class.

IMPORTANT INFORMATION:

THEME: THE GOOD NEWS OF KING JESUS
BIBLE SCRIPTURES: Isaiah 52:7; John 1:6-14

CLASS DEVELOPMENT:

Receive the boys and girls, taking their ages into account. Babies should be placed in cribs, playpens, on blankets or mats — depending on the classroom conditions. Then, welcome all the boys and girls, and indicate where the areas of play and other activities are (this is only for infants from 18 months). In this way, you can make sure that they'll be able to access the previously arranged material in an environment and at a suitable height for their age. This will also allow them to be able to share with their friends and teachers.

At the of the play/activity time, gather all the children together, making a circle to pray and sing some songs to God, thus starting the lesson of the day.

Let's Talk. Start by reminding the children that we've been meeting together for a long time and we've been able to learn beautiful lessons from the Bible in each of our class times. Say: "Doesn't it make you happy when you learn about God and the wonderful work he has done through his Word, the Bible. In the Bible, we learn a very interesting story. It's a story we must never forget; it's about the birth of Jesus, the Son of God. Many years before Jesus was even born, people announced that Jesus would be born. When he arrived, it was a wonderful day."

Let's Play. Gather the children in a circle and sing the song "The B-I-B-L-E." Then teach them the song "Happy Birthday Jesus" (Toddler Worship) by Saddleback Kids. Be sure to encourage all the kids to participate by singing and doing the motions.

Let's Learn. Tell the children that the story of Jesus, the Son of God, was written down many, many years ago, long before Jesus was even born. This Good News was announced to the people through God's prophets and bearers of the Word of God.

Activity. Provide each child with a worksheet. Tell the children to color their worksheets. And then, help them cut out the hearts at the bottom and have them glue a heart on the chest of each child in the picture so that they'll feel like a child of King Jesus.

Conclusion. Thank God for each one of the children who attended class today, and intercede for each one of them.

THE GOOD NEWS OF KING JESUS

JESUS

JESUS

Instructions
Color, then glue a heart on the chest of each child so they'll feel like a child of King Jesus.

LESSON 48: ANNOUNCING THE BIRTH OF JESUS

Biblical Basis:
Matthew 1:18-25; Luke 1:26-56

Objective:
To know that the Bible announces the birth of Jesus.

Class Preparation:
Teachers should meet beforehand to pray for the Class Preparation time. Then carefully read and meditate on the verses listed under the Biblical Basis.

Introduction

Let's think carefully about the following:

Who visited Mary? / What did the angel say to Mary?

What name and title would Jesus carry? / Why did the angel tell Mary about Elizabeth's pregnancy?

Who appeared to Joseph in a dream? / What did the angel say to Joseph?

How did Joseph react to this dream? / Did Joseph quietly divorce Mary according to Jewish law?

Mary was engaged to marry Joseph. They were probably very excited and happy, but they were also observant of the Jewish law. They were just waiting for the wedding day, but something unexpected happened. Mary was surprised when an angel appeared to her and told her that she was going to be a mother, that she would have a son. Right away, the angel indicated what this baby was going to be like, what his name would be, and what he would do for humanity. Mary's reaction was immediate because she knew this wasn't physically possible; but the angel of God told her of the divine work that would take place in her and she believed what she had heard. The angel told her about another incredible event: that her cousin Elizabeth, who was unable to conceive, was pregnant. Mary later visited Elizabeth. The Bible tells us that when Mary visited Elizabeth, upon hearing Mary's voice, Elizabeth's child moved in her womb and Elizabeth was filled by the Holy Spirit and affirmed that Jesus was the Son of God. This was the most important thing that ever happened in history. Joseph, after receiving the news of Mary's pregnancy, was going to divorce Mary according to the law. But he was visited by an angel in a dream and was encouraged to marry her anyway. Because of the words of the angel, he accepted earthly fatherhood and supported Mary until they consummated their marriage after Jesus' birth.

Reflection

- It's important for us to know that God in his eternal wisdom had everything planned! And because of his immense love for mankind, he sent the Savior of the world to save us.
- Pray and thank God for sending his beloved Son to save us from eternal damnation.

At the end of your prayer time, prepare the materials for the upcoming lesson.

IMPORTANT INFORMATION:

THEME: ANNOUNCING THE BIRTH OF JESUS
BIBLE SCRIPTURES: Matthew 1:18-25; Luke 1:26-56

CLASS DEVELOPMENT:

Receive the boys and girls, taking their ages into account. Babies should be placed in cribs, playpens, on blankets or mats — depending on the classroom conditions. Then, welcome all the boys and girls, and indicate where the areas of play and other activities are (this is only for infants from 18 months). In this way, you can make sure that they'll be able to access the previously arranged material in an environment and at a suitable height for their age. This will also allow them to be able to share with their friends and teachers.

At the end of the play/activity time, gather all the children together, making a circle to pray and sing some songs to God, thus starting the lesson of the day.

Let's Talk. Show the children a picture of Mary, the mother of Jesus, and tell the children that today they are going to learn about Mary. She was the mother of Jesus. Ask them if they have heard about Mary before, and let the little ones share what they know about Mary. Listen carefully to what they tell you. Encourage them to say together, "Mary."

Let's Tell the Bible Story: Continue the class by saying: "Mary was a young woman who was engaged to be married to a man named Joseph. Engaged means that she had promised to be married to him. One day, Mary was visited by an angel from heaven who was sent by God. The angel told her that she was going to have a baby and that the baby would be a boy. The angel also told her that she should name the baby Jesus because he would save the world from its sins. At first, Mary was very scared when the angel appeared, but after she heard what the angel said, she was very happy. Since Mary was engaged to Joseph, the angel also visited Joseph as he slept, and the angel told him everything that was going to happen. So Joseph helped Mary with baby Jesus, and Joseph was a good daddy to Jesus."

Let's Play. Organize the boys and girls (try to include all of them) to dramatize the announcement of the birth of Jesus made by the angel to Mary and Joseph. Talk to parents plenty of time before your class and ask them to help you by sending their children to class wearing clothes that resemble the clothes worn during Jesus' time.

Let's Learn. Remind the children that the birth of Jesus, the Son of God, is the most wonderful event that has ever occurred in the history of mankind. It's a story we all should know and share with others.

Activity. Provide a worksheet for each child. Instruct the children to color the picture.

Conclusion. Conclude your class with a prayer, thanking God for sending Jesus, a wonderful gift of love, to us.

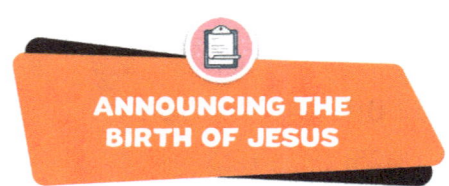
ANNOUNCING THE BIRTH OF JESUS

Instructions

Color the picture of the Angel talking to Mary.

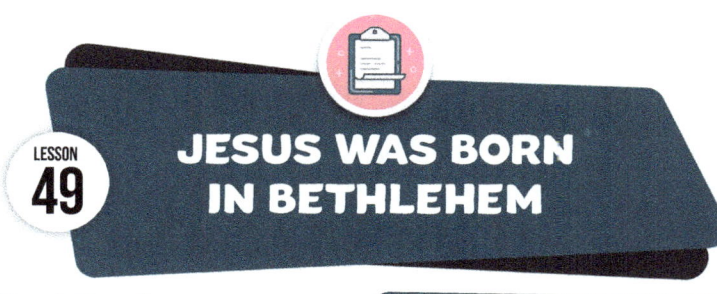

LESSON 49

JESUS WAS BORN IN BETHLEHEM

Biblical Basis:
Luke 2:1-7

Objective:
To know that Jesus was born in Bethlehem, in a humble manger.

Class Preparation:
Teachers should meet beforehand to pray for the Class Preparation time. Then carefully read and reflect on the verses listed under the Biblical Basis.

Introduction

Carefully think about the following:

Who ordered a census throughout the Roman Empire?

Where did Joseph and Mary go to register?

Why did they travel to Bethlehem?

How do you think Mary would have felt during this long trip, considering she was pregnant and about to give birth?

Why wasn't Jesus born in a luxurious palace?

Who are Joseph's ancestors?

The decrees of the Roman government had to be followed; for this reason, everyone had to go to their hometown to register for the census. This was how the empire collected the statistics of its inhabitants so they could collect the corresponding taxes. This was not an easy trip for anyone. Not only did they have to walk many kilometers to get where they had to go, but they also had to carry their own provisions. Mary had to go in spite of her condition because it was the law. And that's how Mary and Joseph ended up in Bethlehem when it was time for Mary to give birth. When they arrived, there was no lodging available, so they were staying in a stable where animals were fed. This was where Jesus was born, thus fulfilling the prophecies. This was God's response to the sins of the world.

Reflection

- We can look with eyes of faith at this great event, the birth of Jesus Christ in a humble manger.
- As we read the details of this wonderful event, we see that just as there was no room for God's little one when he was born; our world has a very similar reaction by denying Jesus a place in their hearts.

Pray that children in your class and their parents will understand the true meaning of the birth of Jesus. At the end of your prayer time, prepare the materials for the following class.

IMPORTANT INFORMATION:

THEME: JESUS WAS BORN IN BETHLEHEM
BIBLE SCRIPTURE: Luke 2:1-7

CLASS DEVELOPMENT:

Receive the boys and girls, taking their ages into account. Babies should be placed in cribs, playpens, on blankets or mats — depending on the classroom conditions. Then, welcome all the boys and girls, and indicate where the areas of play and other activities are (this is only for infants from 18 months). In this way, you can make sure that they'll be able to access the previously arranged material in an environment and at a suitable height for their age. This will also allow them to be able to share with their friends and teachers.

At the end of the play/activity time, gather all the children together, making a circle to pray and sing some songs to God, thus starting the lesson of the day.

Let's Talk. Review the last class with the children saying: "Who visited Mary and Joseph? What did the angel say to them? What were they to name the baby boy? What does the name Jesus mean?" (Allow time for children to remember and respond; then continue.) Say: "Now the time has come and Mary is ready to have her baby. What are some things that the new baby will need?" (Let the children give their answers, some which may be diapers, a shirt, pants, socks, a hat, mittens, a sweater, etc...) "Have you ever seen a newborn baby? Do you have a baby brother or sister at your house? Jesus was born in a place called Bethlehem, and his mommy, Mary, was very happy. She wrapped him up and laid him in a manger. A manger is something that animals eat hay from. Jesus was born in a stable because his mommy and daddy had to take a trip, and there was no place else for them to stay. Jesus' daddy, Joseph, took care of him and loved him very much. Both May and Joseph remembered what the angel told them, and they named him Jesus. His birth was announced by angels, and a very bright star appeared in the sky showing the world that the great King had been born."

Let's Play. Before class time, make some musical instruments (rattles, drums, tambourines, etc.) out of recycled materials, and give one to each child. Sing the song "Oh What a Special Night" by Animated Praise (search YouTube) with all of them.

Let's Learn. Remind the children that Jesus was born in Bethlehem, and he is also in our hearts. We want to be friends with Jesus, so we must pray (talk to him) every day. We sing praises to him and thank him for all the beautiful things he does for us and because we love him.

Activity. Give each child a copy of the worksheet. Explain that they should decorate their picture however they'd like. If possible, provide Christmas colors, stickers, glitter, etc for them to use.

Conclusion. Pray that God will prepare each child's heart to receive him and thank him for the birth of Jesus, our Savior. Stay in touch with the children during week.

JESUS WAS BORN IN BETHLEHEM

Instructions
Decorate the nativity picture.

LESSON 50

THE SHEPHERDS WORSHIPED BABY JESUS

 Biblical Basis:
Luke 2:8-20

 **Objective:**
To know that the shepherds were the first to worship Jesus.

 **Class Preparation:**
Teachers should meet beforehand to pray for the Class Preparation time. Then carefully read and meditate on the verses listed under the Biblical Basis.

Introduction

Let's think carefully about the following:

Where were the shepherds?

How many angels did the shepherds see and what were they doing?

How did the shepherds feel?

What did the shepherds do?

What did the angels tell them?

Where did the shepherds go, according to the angels' directions?

Who did the shepherds tell about what they had seen and heard?

How did Mary feel when the shepherds arrived?

The birth of Jesus was a divine event. God controlled everything, and despite the reality in which he was born, there was great excitement and celebration in heaven like there had never been before. It was not for nothing, for it was the birth of someone very special, the Savior of the world. The angels took part in the celebration and were given the pleasure of announcing the good news, as well as giving directions to the shepherds so that they could worship the newborn Jesus.

Mary, the mother of Jesus, treasured all these things in her heart. This must have been a wonderful experience for Mary. All too soon, the excited and joyful shepherds returned to their fields.

Reflection

We're filled with joy to know that the birth of Jesus not only occurred in a manger but that it can also occur in our hearts. Sadly, sometimes people reject this wonderful fact.

The life of the Christian should be filled with joy and a desire share the good news, not only with the boys and girls that we teach but also with their families and anyone else we encounter.

Pray for the children and their parents, that they'll celebrate this wonderful event of the birth of Jesus our Savior every day.

As you conclude your prayer time, prepare the materials for the upcoming class.

IMPORTANT INFORMATION:

THEME: THE SHEPHERDS WORSHIPED BABY JESUS
BIBLE SCRIPTURE: Luke 2:8-20

CLASS DEVELOPMENT:

Receive the boys and girls, taking their ages into account. Babies should be placed in cribs, playpens, on blankets or mats — depending on the classroom conditions. Then, welcome all the boys and girls, and indicate where the areas of play and other activities are (this is only for infants from 18 months). In this way, you can make sure that they'll be able to access the previously arranged material in an environment and at a suitable height for their age. This will also allow them to be able to share with their friends and teachers.

At the end of the play/activity time, gather all the children together, making a circle to pray and sing some songs to God, thus starting the lesson of the day.

Let's Talk. Review with your class what you talked about last week by saying: "Who did we talk about in the last class? Who was born in Bethlehem? What are the names of Jesus' parents? Where did Mary lay baby Jesus after he was born?" (Allow time for everyone to participate, then continue.) "Jesus was born in Bethlehem. His birth was announced by angels to a group of shepherds who were taking care of their sheep. The Bible tells us that after the shepherds heard the angel's announcement, they quickly went to worship the newborn baby Jesus. His mother, Mary, was very happy."

Let's Play. Show your class some colorful pictures of Jesus, Joseph, and Mary. Then ask them to point out the specific person as you say their name. For example, say "Mary" and have the children point to Mary in the picture. This activity can be done until everyone knows the names of the members of Jesus' family.

Let's Learn. Remind the children that Jesus was born in Bethlehem, and we can ask him into our hearts. When he comes into our hearts, he becomes our friend. We must pray and talk to him everyday because he is our friend and we sing praises to him to thank him for all he does.

Activity. Provide each child with a worksheet and allow them to color it however they'd like. Encourage them to talk about the birth of our Lord Jesus with their friends as they color.

Conclusion. Pray, thanking God for sending his son Jesus; thank Jesus for coming to earth as a baby to save us from our sins.

THE SHEPHERDS WORSHIPED BABY JESUS

Instructions

Color and talk with your friends about the birth of our Lord Jesus.

LESSON 51
THE WISE MEN GAVE PRESENTS TO JESUS

Biblical Basis:
Matthew 2:1-21

Objective:
To know that the Wise men gave valuable gifts to Baby Jesus.

Class Preparation:
Teachers should meet beforehand to pray for the Class Preparation time. Then carefully read and reflect on the verses listed under the Biblical Basis.

Introduction

Let's consider the following:

Who came from the east? / Where did the Wise men go to first?

What were the Wise men looking for?

What did the Wise men see, and whom did they want to worship?

What did Herod do? / Where did Herod send the Wise men?

Where did the star lead the Wise men? / Where did the Wise men return to?

The Wise men, as detailed by Matthew, were sages who had seen a bright star and investigated what the star might mean. They discovered that the star was there to announce the birth of the king of the Jews, but they didn't know exactly where the child was. So they tried to find out more by asking the current king, King Herod. When Herod found out that there was a child born to be king of the Jews, he was upset. He asked the Wise men to find out where the child was and then tell him. The Wise men were guided by the star and found Jesus. They worshiped Baby Jesus and gave him gifts of gold, frankincense, and myrrh. When it was time to return to their country, they were warned in a dream not to return to Herod, so they went home another way.

Reflection

The things that God has shown us are always truly wonderful. He allowed the Savior to be born from the line of David, which had been prophesied, and this news impacted the world at that time. His birth has revolutionized the hearts of those who, because of what they've learned from the Bible, worship the living God and offer their lives to him every day through their obedience and personal witness.

Pray for the children in your class and for their parents, that they'll understand the significance of this event and worship Jesus our Savior.

At the end of your prayer time, prepare the materials for the upcoming class.

IMPORTANT INFORMATION:

THEME: THE WISE MEN GAVE PRESENTS TO JESUS
BIBLE SCRIPTURE: Matthew 2:1-21

CLASS DEVELOPMENT:

Receive the boys and girls, taking their ages into account. Babies should be placed in cribs, playpens, on blankets or mats — depending on the classroom conditions. Then, welcome all the boys and girls, and indicate where the areas of play and other activities are (this is only for infants from 18 months). In this way, you can make sure that they'll be able to access the previously arranged material in an environment and at a suitable height for their age. This will also allow them to be able to share with their friends and teachers.

At the end of the play/activity time, gather all the children together, making a circle to pray and sing some songs to God, thus starting the lesson of the day.

Let's Talk. Show the children pictures of Joseph, Mary, and Jesus, and ask them to remember each of their names. (Always encourage all of the boys and girls to participate, and then continue.)

Let's Tell the Bible Story: Tell today's story by saying: "Do you remember that last week we talked about some shepherds who went to worship the newborn baby Jesus? Today, I want to tell you about some other visitors that went to see baby Jesus. There were some Wise men who lived in another country who studied the stars. They saw a new star in the sky and began to investigate what it might mean. They discovered that the star was there to announce the birth of Jesus, the future king of the Jews. They were guided by a star to Bethlehem. In Bethlehem, they asked King Herod if he knew where they could find the baby, but Herod knew nothing about the baby. He was upset to hear that a baby had been born who would become the king of the Jews instead of him. The Wise men continued to follow the star until they found baby Jesus. When they found Jesus, they worshiped him and gave him gifts of gold, frankincense, and myrrh. King Herod had asked the Wise men to tell him where the baby was because Herod was jealous and wanted to hurt baby Jesus. But the Wise men were warned about the king's plan in a dream, so they returned to their country another way."

Let's Play. Sing with the children the song, "Go-go-go-go Gold!" - Children's Christmas Carol by Maynard's Groovy Bible Tunes or "We Three Kings" by Brentwood Benson (Search YouTube). If you have time, you could also sing one of the other songs you previously sang about Jesus' birth: "Oh What A Special Night" or "Happy Birthday Jesus."

Let's Learn. Tell your students that Jesus, the Son of God, is the most important person in history because he is the King of the whole world. He wants each one of us to love and follow him.

Activity. Give each child a worksheet. Ask the children to tell you what gifts the wise men gave Jesus. Then instruct them to decorate the picture however they like.

Conclusion. Pray, thanking God for the gift of his Son Jesus and for Mary and Joseph, Jesus' parents who took care of him, and for the shepherds and Wise men who went to visit Jesus.

THE WISE MEN GAVE PRESENTS TO JESUS

What were the gifts the Wise men gave to Jesus?

Instructions
Decorate the picture however you would like.

LESSON 52: JESUS, AS A CHILD, RECEIVES PRAISE

Biblical Basis:
Luke 2:21-39

Objective:
To know that Anna and Simeon were able to see Jesus.

Class Preparation:
Teachers should meet beforehand to pray for the Class Preparation time. Then carefully read and meditate on the verses listed under the Biblical Basis.

Introduction

Let's think carefully about the following:

What happened eight days after Jesus was born?

Where did Mary and Joseph take Jesus?

What specifically did they have to do in Jerusalem?

How is Simeon described?   /   Who was Simeon?

How is Anna described?   /   Who was Anna?

What did they do with baby Jesus?

Jesus' family followed the customs and rites of the Jewish people. They did so with their son, Jesus, who at eight days old was presented at the temple to be consecrated to the Lord. Two God-fearing elderly people who were full of the Holy Spirit were also at the temple: Simeon and the prophetess Anna. They were in awe to be able to meet, look at, and hold in their arms the Son of God. To receive the blessing of seeing and holding the child who would become the Messiah was an incredible honor to them.

Reflection

Like Anna and Simeon, we wait for the coming of Christ. Therefore, we must live diligently each day and work without ever losing hope that we will be glorified with our God and Savior.

Pray for the children and their parents. Pray for your team of teachers, that they'll be good teachers of the Word of God and that the children will be taught to serve and worship Jesus the Savior.

IMPORTANT INFORMATION:

THEME: JESUS, AS A CHILD, RECEIVES PRAISE
BIBLE SCRIPTURE: Luke 2:21-39

CLASS DEVELOPMENT:

Receive the boys and girls, taking their ages into account. Babies should be placed in cribs, playpens, on blankets or mats — depending on the classroom conditions. Then, welcome all the boys and girls, and indicate where the areas of play and other activities are (this is only for infants from 18 months). In this way, you can make sure that they'll be able to access the previously arranged material in an environment and at a suitable height for their age. This will also allow them to be able to share with their friends and teachers.

At the end of the play/activity time, gather all the children together, making a circle to pray and sing some songs to God, thus starting the lesson of the day.

Let's Talk. Show the children the pictures of Joseph, Mary, and Jesus (that you used in previous lessons), and ask the children if they remember their names. Then tell them: "When Jesus was eight days old, his parents took him to the temple (or church) to thank God for his birth and to dedicate him to God. That day, at the temple, Mary and Joseph saw an old man named Simeon. Simeon loved God very much. God had promised Simeon that he would see the Messiah before he died. When Simeon saw Mary, Joseph, and Jesus, he took baby Jesus in his arms and thanked God for this blessing. There was also an old woman there who loved God very much. She was always at the temple praying. She, too, came to see baby Jesus and his parents. Her name was Anna. She thanked God for Jesus and talked about Jesus to everyone around her. She told them that Jesus would do great things.

Let's Play. Spend this time singing some of the songs you've taught the children throughout the year. Be sure to use the motions and have fun with the children!

Let's Learn. Tell the children that Jesus was sent by God, and that from a very young age, he was already fulfilling the plan of his heavenly Father.

Activity. Provide a worksheet for each child. Instruct the boys and girls to draw a blue circle around Simeon and draw a red circle around Ana. Then color the picture.

Conclusion. Thank God, encouraging your children to put into practice the things they've learned and to honor Jesus with all of their lives.

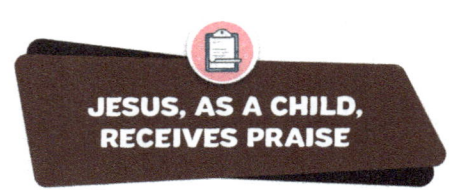

JESUS, AS A CHILD, RECEIVES PRAISE

Instructions

With a blue marker, circle the picture of Simeon, and with a red marker, circle the picture of Anna. Then color the picture.

BIBLIOGRAPHY

- THOMPSON REFERENCE BIBLE

- WORDS OF LIFE SUNDAY SCHOOL LESSONS, 1995

- DISEÑO CURRICULAR NACIONAL DE EDUCACIÓN BÁSICA REGULAR (NATIONAL CURRICULAR DESIGN OF REGULAR BASIC EDUCATION). DINEIP-DINESST 2009

- DISEÑO CURRICULAR REGIONAL DRE PIURA (REGIONAL CURRICULAR DESIGN). 2007

- FRANCISCO TONUCCI: La investigación como alternativa a la enseñanza (Research as an alternative to teaching). 1999

- LEXUS: Libro de la educadora (Educator's Book). 2003

- MINISTERIO DE EDUCACION: Estructura curricular básica de Educación Inicial (MINISTRY OF EDUCATION: Intelligence is built using it).1987

- MINISTERIO DE EDUCACIÓN: La inteligencia se construye usándola. Año 2002

- MINISTERIO DE EDUCACIÓN: Manual de la docente coordinadora y de la Animadora de PRONOEI (MINISTRY OF EDUCATION: Manual of the coordinating teacher and the Animator of PRONOEI). 2001

- MINISTERIO DE EDUCACIÓN: "Calidad y equidad" reglamentación de la Ley General de Educación N° 28044 (MINISTRY OF EDUCATION: "Quality and equity" regulation of the General Education Law No. 28044). 2005

Sunday School / Christian Education Materials for Children

Discipleship Ministries of the Mesoamerica Region presents its complete collection of books on Christian education.

They were designed for children's teachers and for students from 2 to 11 years of age.

Children will learn the lessons of the Bible according to their age. At the end of their elementary school years, they will have gone through the challenging biblical stories as well as various appropriate themes for each stage of their childhood and pre-teenage years.

This material was designed as different steps to achieve a holy life. It contains clear and possible goals.

The teacher's book will help equip those who have the beautiful task of leading children to connect with the message that will change their lives forever.

By promoting the child to the next year of class — according to their age — they will have studied each of the books only once. When they are 12 years old — if they started with the first book — they will have studied the nine books of this valuable collection.

The books were designed to be used in Sunday School, Children's Club, discipleship, and schools in general.

This series aims to:

- Challenge children to learn the Word of God.
- Allow them to grow in their Christian experience as children of God.
- Help them grow in their faith.
- Guide them to accept Jesus as their Savior and Lord.
- Help them to become part of the faith community - the church.

The following will help you identify the appropriate book according to the age of the students:

Nursery Room - 2 and 3 years old (Year / Book 1)

Preschool - 4 and 5 years old (Year / Book 1 and 2).

Elementary - 6 to 8 years old (Year / Book 1, 2, and 3).

Words of Life (pre-adolescents) - 9 to 11 years old (Year / Book 1, 2, and 3).

www.ingramcontent.com/pod-product-compliance
Lightning Source LLC
Chambersburg PA
CBHW050748100426
42744CB00012BA/1936